SCHOOL OF THE FUTURE

SCHOOL OF THE FUTURE

Edited by

WAYNE H. HOLTZMAN

American Psychological Association
and
Hogg Foundation for Mental Health
The University of Texas
Austin, Texas 78713-7998

ISBN 0-943463-11-4

LIST OF CONTRIBUTORS

Harriet Arvey, Ed.D.
Assistant Superintendent of Pupil Services, Houston Independent School District

Marion Tolbert Coleman, Ph.D.
Executive Associate, Hogg Foundation for Mental Health

Hugh F. Crean, B.A.
Research Associate, Hogg Foundation for Mental Health

Ralph E. Culler, Ph.D.
Executive Associate, Hogg Foundation for Mental Health

Rosemary Ellmer, Ph.D.
Project Director, Policy Studies on Texas Children, Institute of Human Development and Family Studies, The University of Texas at Austin

Matia Finn-Stevenson, Ph.D.
Associate Director, The Bush Center in Child Development and Social Policy, Yale University, New Haven

Robert B. Hampson, Ph.D.
Associate Professor of Psychology, Southern Methodist University, Dallas

Wayne H. Holtzman, Ph.D.
President, Hogg Foundation for Mental Health;
Hogg Professor of Psychology and Education, The University of Texas at Austin

Scott S. Keir, Ph.D.
Research Associate, Hogg Foundation for Mental Health

Laura Lein, Ph.D.
Senior Lecturer and Research Scientist, School of Social Work, The University of Texas at Austin

Susan Millea, M.S.W.
Research Associate, Hogg Foundation for Mental Health

Patti Radle, B.A.
Inner-City Development Corporation, San Antonio

Rod Radle, M.S.W.
Program Coordinator, San Antonio School of the Future Project

Kevin D. Stark, Ph.D.
Associate Professor of Educational Psychology, The University of Texas at Austin

Jacqualene J. Stephens, Ph.D.
Department of Psychology, The University of Texas Southwestern Medical Center at Dallas

Allen R. Sullivan, Ph.D.
Executive Director, Student Support Services, Dallas Independent School District

Deborah J. Tharinger, Ph.D.
Associate Professor of Educational Psychology, The University of Texas at Austin

Margaret C. Wang, Ph.D.
Director, Center for Research in Human Development and Education, Temple University, Philadelphia

TABLE OF CONTENTS

FOREWORD

The past decade has been marked by a growing awareness that American education faces many critical problems. The findings of a recent survey by the American Association for the Advancement of Science, projecting catastrophic shortfalls in scientists, engineers, and technicians by the mid-1990s, gives cause for serious concern. Consequently, helping students to develop academic competence, especially in science and mathematics, is essential for the United States to remain competitive in an increasingly technological, information-oriented global society.

Symptoms of the problems in American education can also be seen in the results of recent studies which show that a substantial proportion of high school graduates lack the basic skills needed to perform adequately in occupations requiring only modest proficiency in mathematics. Typical U.S. eighth graders rank twelfth in mathematical achievement among students in 18 leading industrialized nations, and even those who are enrolled in the most advanced high school math courses score below the average of students from 15 other industrialized nations. The problems in American education are especially critical for at-risk minority students who will comprise nearly 40 percent of our school age population as we enter the 21st Century.

Critics who place exclusive blame on our public schools for the current deficiencies in American education clearly oversimplify the basis for these problems. Social changes within American society have resulted in a substantial increase in the number of children living in poverty, in single-parent families, and in families where both parents work. Child neglect and drug abuse are also rampant in many communities.

What can be done to help American children acquire the knowledge and skills that will be needed to respond to the challenges of an ever-changing society in communities beset by drugs, disrupted family structure, poverty and homelessness, and child abuse and neglect? This volume provides a cogent analysis of the many factors that contribute to the problems in American education. In addition, exciting new approaches to improving education that integrate health care with mental health and family services with educational programs at the neighborhood school level are described.

The experimental School of the Future programs developed in four Texas cities, with consultation and financial support from the Hogg Foundation for Mental Health, have great potential for contributing to educational improvement and school reform. These programs incorporate the best features of previous community-based school interventions that have proved highly successful. They recognize and fulfill the critical need for strong commitment of school administrators and community leaders, the active involvement of teachers and parents, and the cooperation of community agencies that provide vital family services.

The establishment of the School of the Future programs in Austin, Dallas, Houston, and San Antonio follows an intensive examination of the mental health needs of Texas children, adolescents, and their families by three statewide commissions convened in 1987 by the Hogg Foundation. It was the general consensus of these commissions that the Foundation should undertake a major long-term demonstration project that focused on child development, family preservation, and community renewal. The Foundation's establishment of the School of the Future programs was supported by a long-term commitment of $2 million over an initial five-year period.

Through a constructive partnership with public and private community organizations and agencies, the School of the Future programs enhance the educational process by providing for the coordination and delivery of a broad spectrum of health and human services. Intensive pre-implementation planning by the Hogg Foundation staff takes into account the utopian vision of the School of the 21st Century as proposed by Edward Zigler and his associates at Yale University and the community-oriented educational intervention programs developed by James Comer in New Haven that emphasized mental health support at the elementary school level. The Foundation staff has also worked constructively and nonintrusively with community leaders and assisted them in evolving their own governance structures and in establishing comprehensive programs that optimally integrate the unique strengths and resources of each community.

The Hogg Foundation's School of the Future programs are based on a cohesive, integrated community approach to serving the educational, health care, mental health, and social needs of children and their families, with the neighborhood school as the focus of the delivery of needed services. The Foundation's comprehensive studies of the mental health needs of Texas citizens, the intensive planning that preceded launching the School of the Future project, and the long-term commitment to provide financial support and consultation on program development and evaluation are especially commendable. High quality staff consultation and continuing financial support will, no doubt, be key factors for ensuring the success of these vital programs.

No less important is the effort invested by the Foundation staff in identifying schools, neighborhoods, and communities that were willing to undertake the demanding effort of developing School of the Future programs and helping these groups to recruit talented staff to carry them out. The early achievements of these programs provide ample evidence that a true partnership has been established between parents, teachers, school administrators, participating community agencies, and the Foundation staff. The involvement of parents and teachers in all aspects of the programs appears to be a critical factor for their success. From the reports in this volume, this involvement has been strongly established and is likely to continue.

Although the School of the Future programs are at an early stage of development, they have already demonstrated the importance for educational reform of integrating health care with mental health and social services with educational programs at the community neighborhood level. Educators and health care and mental health specialists are already greatly indebted to the Hogg Foundation for its pioneering work in the planning, implementation, and evaluation of what promises to be one of the most important demonstration projects in the history of American education. We are also indebted to Professor Wayne H. Holtzman, president of the Foundation, for his dedicated leadership in developing the School of the Future programs and for stimulating his colleagues to contribute chapters to this volume in which they share with us their expertise and experience.

Charles D. Spielberger, *President*
American Psychological Association

INTRODUCTION

by

Wayne H. Holtzman

For more than a hundred years, major waves of educational reform have periodically swept across the American landscape. The most recent reform effort began about 15 years ago, rising to the level of national debate during the 1980s. The perceived failure of public education to turn out highly skilled, knowledgeable graduates who would continue to assure America's preeminence in commerce, industry, science, and technology was the dominant theme of the early Reagan administration, as exemplified in 1983 by the book *A Nation at Risk*.[1] Disillusionment with the major social and educational reforms of the 1960s, followed by the economic disruptions of the 1970s and the major shift in federal policies during the 1980s under the Reagan administration, focused attention upon public education as a scapegoat for much of the social distress apparent throughout the country.

The subsequent calls for school improvement were backed by little additional money. Indeed, federal funds during the 1980s for elementary and secondary education declined 17 percent, after adjusting for inflation.[2] Similarly, while total funding for federal research and development, particularly in defense, increased steadily during the 1980s, federal support of educational research and development decreased by 33 percent.[3] State and local sources of support were expected during this period to make up the difference not only in the funding of education but also in many other areas of health and human services. Accompanying this massive decline in federal support is the rise in the proportion of children living in poverty from 15 to 20 percent. This large rise is only partly explained by the extraordinary increase in single-parent families. The United States now has the highest child poverty rate of the six leading industrialized countries, but ranks only third in single-parent families. It spends a lower amount of our gross national product on income support for children than do any of the other highly industrialized countries.

National statistics paint a grim outlook for many children and adolescents today. If a child is born to a single mother, chances are one in two that she or he will live in poverty. Among teenage parents seven out of ten are living in poverty. As many as 12 million American children have no health insurance. Many live with the threat of violence on a daily basis. Every day more than 1,500 youngsters drop out of school. Of those who stay in school, studies repeatedly show that about half graduate with inadequate basic skills to perform moderately well in modern society.[4] Statistical trends such as these have been well publicized, raising national awareness of the urgent need for more enlightened public policies and support that reflect the vital importance of community renewal, family preservation, child development, and education. No longer is the debate concerned with the validity of these ominous social trends or with who is to blame for the nation's problems. Attention is now being focused upon what reforms to undertake and how they can best be accomplished, not whether they are needed in the first place.

Most observers now firmly believe that major reform in public education, perhaps even radical changes that would scarcely have been voiced a generation ago, will be the primary driving force to ameliorate these social problems. Psychologists and other behavioral scientists can be in the forefront of bringing about the necessary changes and scientific advancement for such reforms to succeed. It is highly likely that the next decade will see an ever-increasing involvement of psychologists, sociologists, anthropologists, economists, and social workers. They will be joining forces with educational specialists, not only in the research and development aspects of educational reform but also in the social engineering of major field experiments, model schools, and policy studies that will provide the basis for effective reforms.

Particularly promising are recent projects demonstrating ways in which traditional education can be integrated with a wide array of health and human services, both treatment and prevention, for which the school is becoming the locus of delivery. This larger vision of the school of the future, not only as a place for academic learning but also as the primary neighborhood institution for promoting child and family development, has profound implications for community renewal, family preservation, and the nature of delivery systems for health, human services, and education.

In 1989, when the professional staff and advisers of the Hogg Foundation for Mental Health began discussing the concept of the school of the future, we soon realized that a comprehensive project of this magnitude would require many partners and millions of dollars to ensure its success. At the same time, it became apparent that an undertaking of this kind would fulfill many of the long-term objectives of the Foundation. Unlike any other private foundation, the Hogg Foundation for Mental Health is an integral part of a major state university, The University of Texas, that is sustained largely with public funds. The Foundation's program of activities is supported entirely by a major endowment given the University by the children of Governor James Hogg. Since 1940 the Foundation has carried out a mandate to initiate and support mental health programs to benefit all the people of Texas. Most of its $3 million annual budget is used to provide grants to nonprofit organizations throughout Texas. Proposals are reviewed continuously by a staff of seven highly qualified professionals, all of whom also spend a great deal of time providing technical assistance to grant recipients and other agencies. A small number of mental health research projects have been developed and directed by Foundation officers themselves. Consisting primarily of psychologists and sociologists, most of the professional staff of the Foundation teach some advanced classes and seminars within the University.

Special emphasis is given in the Foundation to innovative community mental health programs that have systematic evaluation as an essential part of the project design. Doctoral candidates in the behavioral sciences augment the permanent Foundation staff by serving, under the direction of senior program officers, as evaluation research fellows and research associates on community projects. Over the past 21 years as president of the Foundation, I have been allowed to set aside a small amount of unused money each year as a reserve fund for future use should an opportunity arise that would justify major expenditures beyond the normal budget. In the past few years this fund has grown to several million dollars, an amount sufficient to embark on a bold new venture.

During the 1980s the Foundation began to take an increasingly active role in addressing significant problems of the day, following suggestions made by its National Advisory Council. Three statewide commissions were appointed in 1987 to focus upon three areas of great concern to the Foundation—community care of the mentally ill, the mental health of children and their families, and the mental health issues confronting adolescents and young adults. As the work of these commissions came to a climax in 1989, a general consensus was reached that the Foundation could best contribute to the human development of Texas, as well as the rest of the nation, by undertaking a major long-term project to demonstrate an effective approach to community renewal, family preservation, and child development.

Established initially in four Texas cities—Austin, San Antonio, Houston, and Dallas—the School of the Future is supported by major Hogg Foundation resources including an initial five-year commitment totaling about $2 million. Involving school personnel, parents, community volunteers, and enlisting the aid of dozens of organizations concerned about children in each community, the School of the Future is an ongoing program that captures the original vision of Miss Ima Hogg, the Foundation's benefactor, and her lifelong commitment on behalf of children.

Part 1 of this book deals with the concept of the School of the Future as a community institution, how it fits into the national scene, and plans for evaluation. Chapter 1 begins with a review of school-based services and continues with a description of successful experiments recently completed. The School of the Future is then presented in some detail, drawing in a comprehensive manner upon these earlier projects. Plans for evaluating the impact of the programs upon the children, teachers, parents, and the community itself are described in chapters 2 and 3. Chapter 2 focuses primarily upon qualitative data collected from interviews that explore the realities behind education and the social service reforms. This process evaluation should prove especially valuable in understanding the complex evolution of the School of the Future at each site, the political realities that are ever present, and the factors that must be given priority when implementing a major program of this magnitude. The design for evaluating the outcome of specific programs upon the thousands of school children involved is presented in chapter 3, where special attention is given to the collection of baseline data in the initial phase of the project in order that extensive longitudinal studies across the four sites could be undertaken five years later.

In chapter 4, Matia Finn-Stevenson of Yale University compares certain features of the School of the Future with programs elsewhere, especially Edward L. Zigler's vision of the School of the 21st Century, which emphasizes the need for schools everywhere to focus more on preschool education while providing continuity of child care. A number of questions concerning unresolved issues in the full implementation of the School of the Future are raised, together with a discussion of criteria by which both the process and outcome can be evaluated.

In the last chapter of part 1, Margaret Wang of Temple University presents a comprehensive view of factors that must be considered in the design and evaluation of major programs such as the School of the Future. Recognizing the primary goals of schooling, she then presents a conceptual model of variables that are important to learning and suggests ways in which they can be built into program design and evaluation.

Part 2 is devoted to the models of intervention that are emerging in each of the four communities where the School of the Future is being developed. As described in chapter 6, the San Antonio program is in the center of the oldest public housing project in the United States, a traditional Mexican-American neighborhood that is both proud and poor, having existed as a barrio for over a hundred years. Houston's School of the Future is described in chapter 7. The elementary and middle schools are in a dynamically changing neighborhood called The Heights—a rapidly growing, predominantly Hispanic area which still has some older African-American families. Unlike the other three sites where the Hogg Foundation's support was granted directly to the public school systems, in Houston a private, nonprofit agency, the Family Service Center, is the principal agent through which reform is taking place in close partnership with the schools.

Chapter 8 tells the story of the Dallas School of the Future, which is being viewed by the central school administration as a model for dynamic change throughout the system. An emphasis upon wellness and the empowerment of parents, as well as special training of teachers, is receiving primary attention in this predominantly African-American neighborhood of South Dallas where the elementary schools are built into a converted shopping center. The Austin project, as described in chapter 9, focuses primarily on creating a sense of community in a neighborhood where previously none existed. The Dove Springs area of South Austin is a relatively new but isolated part of the city which has been adversely affected by the recent economic recession. Austin is also the site for a new initiative by The University of Texas and its doctoral program in school psychology where a special partnership has been developed with the School of the Future to provide advanced student training, research, and services for at-risk and emotionally disturbed children, as described in chapter 10.

The final chapter of the book contains a brief look to the future that recognizes the unfinished nature of the comprehensive demonstration project now under way.

As in any large-scale, multidisciplinary project with many partners, the School of the Future owes a debt of gratitude to numerous individuals in The University of Texas, as well as within each of the four communities where the experimental program has been established.

The success of the School of the Future thus far as a demonstration project owes a great debt of gratitude to many individuals who have contributed significantly to its development during the past two years. The authors wish to thank especially Charles M. Bonjean, Adrian R. Fowler, Reymundo Rodríguez, Bert Kruger Smith, Mary T. Banks, Pam Diamond, Tracy Levins, Dorinda Noble, Ines Poza-Juncal, Mary Sondgeroth, and Gayle Vincent of the central staff of the Hogg Foundation; the coordinators of site activities and their close professional associates including Víctor Rodríguez, David Splitek, Joe Nick Garza, Henry Ziegler, Rachel Peña, and Diego Gallegos in San Antonio, Marilyn Rangel, Glenda Stover, and David Duty in Austin, Ruth Turner, Marcia Booker, Truman Thomas, Lenore Stephens, and Wanda Smith in Dallas, and Alfredo Tijerina, Lloyd Sidwell, and Pamela Orpinas in Houston; and our colleagues on the Evaluation Review Committee—G. Edward Codina (San Antonio), Jay R. Cummings (Austin), George W. Holden (Austin), James A. Johnson, Jr. (Austin), and Guy Parcel (Houston). Especially important as participants are the principals, teachers, and staff in the participating schools, as well as the parent leaders and school board members, participating health and human service agencies, and representatives of corporate sponsors from the communities, without whom this project would not be possible. Although they are too numerous to mention by name, it is obvious that the future of this program lies in the hands of the parents, teachers, and the children themselves. And last, we wish to thank Ida Fisher, who assisted with typing and editorial work throughout the production and revision of manuscripts for this book.

WHH

Notes

[1] U.S. National Commission on Excellence in Education, *A nation at risk.* (Washington, DC: 1983).

[2] National Center for Education Statistics, *Federal support for education: Fiscal years 1980 to 1989.* (Washington, DC: U.S. Department of Education, 1990).

[3] E. R. House, "Big policy, little policy," *Educational Researcher.* (1991): 21–26.

[4] Children's Defense Fund, *S.O.S. America! A Children's Defense Fund budget.* (Washington, DC: 1990).

PART 1

CHAPTER 1

Community Renewal, Family Preservation, and Child Development Through the School of the Future

by

Wayne H. Holtzman

As a result of large-scale social changes and the immigration of ethnic minorities to major cities, most of the metropolitan public school districts have heavy concentrations of disadvantaged students. The life chances of these children are seriously hampered by emerging new norms fostering out-of-wedlock childbearing, dropping out of school, joblessness, and other negative outcomes. These social changes have placed unusually heavy burdens upon public education in the past two decades, leading to emotional distress, poor morale, and difficult learning conditions in many inner-city schools.

Alarmed about the future prospects of society without reform, large multinational private corporations such as Eastman Kodak and IBM and many groups of parents and other private citizens have expressed a renewed determination to get involved and make a real difference in contributing to a better society. Business and industry now realize that unless they can find an effective way to build a modern, highly educated, skilled work force on a multicultural basis that includes all Americans, the future prospects of the country are indeed grim.

The steady rise in the prevalence and severity of social problems for children, youth, and families during the past several decades has been accompanied by a great increase in the number of organizations and agencies created to deal with them. Public or private, large or small, comprehensive or focusing only on single issues, such organizations within each of our major metropolitan areas now number in the many hundreds. Government programs with a bewildering array of regulations have contributed to the severe fragmentation of services. Many of these human services are seriously underfunded, often desperately changing course in order to obtain renewed funding for survival.

A conservative estimate of just the public agencies outside of education which are serving youth puts the total in America at more than 21,000. California alone attempts to serve children and youth through more than 160 publicly funded state programs in the 35 agencies and state departments (Kirst, McLaughlin, & Massell, 1990). While it is easy to understand how all these different programs arise in response to specific problems, the resulting fragmentation and inefficiency leads to a chaotic and frustratingly inadequate system of service delivery. Social problems rarely exist in isolation. Children suffering from child abuse, for example, are likely to experience other problems in their homes, such as family involvement in substance abuse and inadequate parental supervision. The result is that clients must be referred to various agencies, usually in different locations, thus wasting a great deal of time and money while discouraging the would-be client. A coordinated approach that integrates many services in one accessible neighborhood location, including referral and follow-up, is far more likely to be effective.

Advantages of School-Based Services

Using the school as a locus of delivery for primary health care, child care, preschool and parent education, recreation, and family counseling, as well as for traditional educational activities, offers many advantages. School facilities are generally underutilized except during traditional school hours. Early mornings, late afternoons, evenings, and weekends, the school's physical plant could be available for meetings, presentations, treatment, and many other community uses. Of course it would take some additional resources to maintain the physical plant and perhaps to modify or expand it for most effective integration of such activities, but the minor extra cost would pay big dividends in parent involvement, school climate, and community support of education. Much of the financing could be arranged through joint venture with the other nonprofit agencies participating in the programs. Any necessary expansion can take form in adjacent properties rather than squeezing programs more tightly within the traditional school building. Many schools are already moving in this direction, while others are debating how much transformation would be required.

A second major advantage of using the school as the locus of service delivery is the identification of children in need and the provision of outreach services. Children are observed daily in school, and often their appearance and behavior provide indications of problems at home. Teachers can be a good source for identifying youngsters in need of help as well as promoting the effectiveness of services that have been provided.

A third advantage of school-based services is the fact that in many neighborhoods the school is the only stable social institution serving the entire community. Broadening the range of services with a focus upon child and family development will enhance the image of the school within the community. Already, in many cases, parents and children get to know and respect their school principals, counselors, and teachers, often turning to school personnel for advice about medical, psychological, financial, and other noneducational problems. In any case, an improved image can enable schools to serve their students better.

Still a fourth advantage of a one-stop comprehensive human service program for many low-income families is the fact that obtaining transportation to single-purpose programs scattered across the city ranges from difficult to impossible. Placing such programs in or adjacent to neighborhood schools, which are frequently located within easy walking distance from students' homes, can greatly help to alleviate this problem.

An example of how this can work for adolescents is the school-based youth services program developed in 1987 by the New Jersey Department of Human Services (Palaich, Whitney, & Paolino, 1991). The program is a unique collaboration of schools and social service agencies which provide "one-stop shopping" for primary and preventive health care, mental health resources, employment counseling, tutorial help, and recreation.

School-based health clinics represent a different kind of community partnership for youth. Currently 18 projects in 15 cities across the country are receiving support from the Robert Wood Johnson Foundation to establish school-based health services for adolescents at risk for serious sociomedical problems (Porter, 1990). The Denver school-based health care program under the University of Colorado Health Sciences Center is a good example of such a school-based clinic. In the 1989–90 school year, students from three Denver high schools in which the pilot clinics operate made 7,646 visits to the clinics for a wide range of health problems (Guernsey, 1990). Since parental consent must be obtained in order to use the services, the families themselves are drawn close to the schools.

Many metropolitan school systems already have a long list of human services available to students on selected campuses, but they are not socially integrated or comprehensive in the way they are delivered. All too frequently they are available only at certain campuses, making access difficult for children and families from other parts of the city. Usually they are single-purpose and funded by outside resources that are limited to a specific purpose such as drug abuse prevention or vision and hearing testing. Typical of such programs is the list of services available to the students within the Austin, Texas, public schools. Of nearly 60 different programs, about one-third deal with mental health and human services. These range from Communities in Schools for dropout prevention to the Drug Abuse Resistance Education (DARE) program. Services of this kind that are highly valued by both the school personnel and the families they serve are likely to grow and eventually be effectively integrated, providing further justification for their incorporation as part of the school of the future.

Comer's School Development Program

One of the most successful and widely publicized school improvement programs was begun by James Comer and his colleagues in the New Haven public schools in 1968 (Comer, 1980). Often referred to as either the Comer Model or the School Development Program, this model went through an initial developmental period until 1975 when the program was firmly enough established that it could be adequately documented and evaluated. The program places a heavy emphasis upon a mental health approach for dealing with problems at the elementary school level. Four major components provide the main thrust of the program—a government and management team, a mental health team, a parent participation program, and a program for curriculum and staff development.

The management team typically consists of seven adults—two elected teachers, three parents appointed by the parent organization, a mental health team member, and the school principal, who serves as leader of the team. Meeting on a weekly basis, the management group establishes policy guidelines, carries out systematic planning and evaluation, coordinates the work of all the participants in the school, and helps the parent group in planning its activities. The group is trained to reach decisions by consensus, and members focus specifically on improving school climate.

The mental health team comprises a classroom teacher, a special education teacher, a school psychologist, and a social worker. The group meets weekly in a clinical case conference to deal with children referred by teachers or parents. Direct counseling, consultation, or referral for specialized services typically follows the clinical case conference. In addition, the mental health team provides training for school personnel in child development and mental health, often advising the management group where school policy and practice can be improved to prevent future problems.

The parent participation program consists of three sequential levels of participation: (1) broad-based activities for a large number of parents; (2) parents working on about a one-to-one ratio with professional staff as classroom assistants, tutors, or aides; and (3) a small number of highly involved parents participating in school government. Consultation and material resources are provided by project staff at all three levels.

The fourth component consists of curriculum and development activities led by the management team. A mental health approach is integrated wherever possible into curriculum planning. Teachers participate in monthly seminars and work closely with curriculum specialists. Two areas of focus are basic skill instruction in reading and mathematics and a social skills curriculum designed to improve self-concept and to enable children to cope more successfully with mainstream American society.

The performance of children, the morale of teachers, the school climate, and the amount of community involvement in the school improved dramatically after several years within the two experimental schools. Nearly all of the children were from families with low income, and 98 percent were African-American. Initially, pupils in these schools were among the lowest in academic achievement compared to the other 29 elementary schools in New Haven. Since 1975, fourth-grade students at King Elementary School who initially had ranked at or near the bottom in reading and mathematics have moved ahead of students at all other inner-city schools. School attendance was consistently near the top, and teacher attendance was the best in the New Haven school system. By 1987, most parents were deeply involved in their children's education. In that year, 92% of the parents visited the school 10 times or more (Comer, 1988).

Before the Comer Model was established, the school staff felt abandoned, parents felt cut off from the school, and community workers complained that the schools did not create the kind of self-esteem needed for academic achievement. The Yale Child Study Center Mental Health Team, which established the model and provided leadership for the experimental program in New Haven, consisted of a child psychiatrist (Comer), two social workers, an early childhood educator, a teacher-trainer, and a psychologist.

In the past 10 years, more than 50 schools nationwide have adopted various aspects of the Comer Model. Among the more successful are those that followed faithfully the key components and guiding philosophy of the basic model that was developed in New Haven. For example, the public schools in Benton Harbor, Michigan, adopted the school development program in 1981 under court orders as part of a remedy to improve the local school climate and academic conditions. A small city, Benton Harbor was severely depressed economically, and "white flight" had shifted the demographics until African-Americans comprised 80 percent of the student population. Four schools were selected initially for phase one, followed later by three more schools in phase two, making possible comparative studies of change due to the implementation of the Comer Model. Results were fairly striking. While the district as a whole experienced an increase in behavior problems, suspensions decreased for the program schools as did absenteeism and corporal punishment, which dropped from 134 incidents in the baseline year to none two years later. Even more important was the finding that the percentage of pupils obtaining at least 75 percent of the objectives on the Michigan Educational Assessment Program, a statewide competency test at the fourth-grade level in mathematics and reading, also increased markedly over the four-year period (Haynes, Comer, & Hamilton-Lee, 1988).

One of the features of the Comer Model that has attracted many concerned citizens across the country is the extent to which parents are empowered through school involvement, leading to other school reforms. The term "restructuring" is now being used by many groups to mean the wholesale reorganization of schools, particularly site-based management. What this means in practice varies widely, but the fact that the principal, teachers, and parents learn to work closely together in building a common consensus within the Comer Model is particularly attractive to advocates of "restructuring." A special report in *Fortune* magazine (Perry, 1989) emphasized the importance of "restructuring" as a way of helping America's schools. In some cases entire communities are being mobilized as in Chelsea, Massachusetts, which has asked Boston University to take care of the management of its public schools as a way of bringing about major change. The school board contributes space and pays for extra services and utilities in order that the physical plant can operate from six in the morning until six in the evening throughout the year.

Child Care and Family Support Services

Formal schooling in most societies generally begins at the age of five or six. By the time children are ready for such schooling, they have already completed what is probably the most important period of learning, growth, and development in their lives, the early formative years during which the family and home environment are most crucial. Among the many projects dealing with early childhood intervention that were undertaken in the early 1970s were three major parent-child development research centers—one in Detroit associated with the Merrill Palmer School, a second in a poor African-

American area of Alabama, and a third for impoverished Mexican-American children in the city of Houston. All three were aimed at developing experimental programs to improve parent-child relations and to make better teachers out of parents, beginning at the birth of the child and continuing to the age of three when the child would be eligible for enrollment in the national system of Head Start programs.

The Houston Center under the leadership of Dale Johnson, a psychologist at the University of Houston, developed a long-term program involving more than seven hundred very young Mexican-American children and their parents (Johnson & Breckenridge, 1982). Each year for eight years nearly one hundred families were assigned randomly to either experimental or control groups. Initial contact was made with mothers immediately after their children's births. Periodic home contacts were maintained for the first 12 months, introducing the mother to a number of techniques for intellectual stimulation of the child. The mother was coached in her communications with the child in order to promote cognitive and personality growth while maintaining strong affectional bonds with her child. Both mother and father, as well as brothers and sisters, were included in the program. The techniques were carefully adapted to the cultural milieu in which the family lived.

When a child was two years old, mother and child attended a special nursery school four mornings a week. Videotaped recordings of mother-child interactions were played back for the mother in order that she could see where she was facilitating or inhibiting desired behavior in the child.

Families placed in the control groups were contacted periodically and had some group meetings but no intensive training of mothers or follow-up activities, as in the experimental group. Johnson continued to follow these children, many of whom then enrolled in the Head Start program in Houston. Grants from the Spencer Foundation and the Hogg Foundation for Mental Health made it possible for him to retest these children years later when in the fourth grade and again as young adolescents. The results of his studies are informative.

Differences between experimental and control children on standardized intelligence tests were generally minor or insignificant. Differences in other measures, however, were striking. Children whose mothers had gone through the special training program and had participated in the parent-child program for two years when the children were very young showed far fewer behavioral problems, higher motivation to succeed, better grades in school, and higher self-esteem than did the control cases who did not participate in the special program.

Early Parent Education

Today, most developmental psychologists and educators are convinced that child care and early childhood intervention involving special parental training are essential for children who come from poor environments, if the children are to succeed in school and become productive, healthy citizens in modern society. Psychologists have been at the forefront of research and program development in this rapidly growing field. Many of the great social experiments conducted in the early child development research centers and within Head Start have now been sufficiently well evaluated to raise our confidence that social competence, cognitive ability, self-esteem, and mental health can be significantly improved by special programs for young children. While most of the major experiments such as the Houston Parent-Child Development Project were very expensive, in recent years inexpensive, more cost-effective programs have been launched. Among the leaders in this field is an educational program for young parents called "Parents as Teachers" (Meyerhoff & White, 1986).

Young mothers just prior to the birth of their firstborn are particularly receptive to guidance in parenting. The state of Missouri developed a pilot program demonstrating that group meetings and home visits for parents beginning in the third trimester of pregnancy and lasting until the young child is three years old will result in significant improvement of the child's intellectual, social, and moral development. The program has been so successful that a national center has been established in Missouri to provide training, technical assistance, and research opportunities for professionals who are interested in this model program. Developed under the leadership of Burton White, a psychologist who headed the Harvard Preschool Project, the program was first extensively tested in a suburb of St. Louis. Today, all school districts in Missouri must offer at least some early learning services under the Parents as Teachers program. All parents with children younger than age three are eligible, but participation is voluntary. Special efforts are made to reach out to high-risk, poor families. The program has now spread to 28 states including Texas, which has new programs in more than 21 cities.

Trained parent-educators conduct group meetings and make home visits to prospective mothers prior to the birth of their infants. Using specially developed curriculum materials and homemade educational toys, the educators increase the parents' knowledge about child development and positive parenting strategies. Parental attitudes about child rearing are changed as the parents take on the role of teachers for their own young children. The program is based on the belief that parents who experience this training will have children who demonstrate increased cognitive functioning, accelerated language development, and a greater sense of self-confidence at three years of age. In addition to the monthly private visits in the home by parent-educators, parents receive practical information and guidance and participate in monthly and group meetings for parents with similarly aged children.

Many public schools have already incorporated Head Start or other similar preschool programs as part of the regular curriculum for children from low-income families. Extending these activities downward by adding a program such as Parents as Teachers is a logical next step in providing continuity of child development from birth on through the school years. In many cities the schools will be the best place within which to develop these essential family support services.

Zigler's School of the 21st Century

The number of families with no adults at home during the working day has increased greatly in the past several decades, creating an urgent national need for good-quality day care services throughout the country. The problem is particularly acute for low-income families in which both parents work or for single parents who are largely living in poverty and cannot afford private day care. As many observers have pointed out, the unmet child care needs in America have become a national scandal that must be corrected. While politicians debate various philosophies and formulas for addressing this problem, Edward Zigler and his associates in the Bush Center in Child Development and Social Policy at Yale University have proposed a unified system of child care and family support using the public schools as the locus of services (Zigler, 1989; Zigler & Lang, 1991). Working from the fundamental principle that all children must have access to stable, good-quality child care when and if they need it and that such care should not be dependent upon family income, ethnicity, or the neighborhood in which they happen to live, they propose that child care be built into the elementary school systems of the nation at all levels.

Zigler's vision of the School of the 21st Century would make use where possible of available school buildings and would provide a variety of child care and family support services. Many of these activities are already provided but delivered in piecemeal fashion. Incorporating them into a comprehensive child care and family support system under the auspices of the public school would involve several major components. First would be an all-day, year-round child care program for preschoolers from age three to kindergarten, a program not unlike existing Head Start programs in many communities. A second component would consist of child care from kindergarten to at least grade six, before and after school and during vacation periods. Three other components would comprise outreach services to benefit all families—a network of family day care providers, a resource and referral system, and a home-based family support and parent education program.

The concept is sufficiently flexible to allow adaptation from one community to the next within the broad principles that comprise good-quality day care. Sliding-scale fees, parental choice, and continuity of child development from prenatal to adolescence are among the more attractive features of the plan. While not yet fully implemented in any major community, prototype pilot programs are under way in a number of schools. In Independence County, Missouri, for example, a school-based program supported primarily by parental fees for service was established in 1988.

The Independence School District offers the program in all 11 elementary schools for children three to six years old and has provided a preschool child care component for all families in the district, using the Parents as Teachers program adopted statewide. Information and referral services, combined with an outreach program for all family day care providers, have also been implemented as additional components in Independence. The Independence program and three similar ones in Connecticut are now being systematically evaluated by Zigler and Matia Finn-Stevenson from the Yale Bush Center.

Experimental Prototype of the School of the Future

Each of the successful programs mentioned above—Comer's School Development Program, Zigler's School of the 21st Century emphasizing child care and family support services, and the more specific programs for community renewal, family preservation, and child development using the school as the primary locus of services—has gained national attention. They are cited for improving school climate; reducing dropouts; improving achievement levels, social behavior, and self-esteem of students; improving teacher morale; and increasing the involvement of parents and other community members in the educational enterprise. The results are sufficiently promising, especially for inner-city schools in low-income neighborhoods, to justify a major effort devoted to a comprehensive experimental program covering the full range of proven innovations appropriate for children from birth to adolescence.

Such an experimental "school of the future" must be implemented and supported for many years with an emphasis upon longitudinal evaluation of the children's development, of teaching and learning activities, of school organizations, of community renewal, and of family growth and development. Ample planning time and resources must be provided to assure the successful implementation of the key components for schools of the future. Baseline data must be collected initially from children and families within the neighborhood of the school if change is to be studied systematically. The process and decision-making characteristic of the implementation effort must be adequately documented, analyzed, and interpreted if the experiment is to be of use for others interested in replicating the program. Essential features for such a school of the future would have to be recognized and enthusiastically accepted by all stakeholders in the program—school personnel, parents, community leaders, human service providers, educational specialists, and behavioral scientists concerned with model building and evaluation. Sufficient resources would have to be provided on an indefinite basis to assure the long-range viability of the plan.

National advisers to the Hogg Foundation encouraged staff to plan for a major new initiative aimed at helping children and their families cope more successfully with the difficult circumstances in which many find themselves. After many preliminary discussions with community leaders, school administrators, mental health professionals, and national advisers, the concept of the school of the future was announced as the most ambitious initiative the Hogg Foundation has undertaken in its 50 years of existence.

Key Elements of Program Design

Months of initial planning in each of four metropolitan areas—Austin, San Antonio, Houston, and Dallas—led to selection of elementary and middle schools to become the sites for the experimental program. Initial grants from the Foundation of $50,000 per year for five years—a total of $1,000,000—were committed in the spring of 1990, making it possible for each of the communities to appoint a full-time project coordinator. An equal amount of money has been set aside to provide each site with technical assistance and evaluation support. Community agencies and private corporations have joined the Foundation and the school systems as partners in support of the program. Five essential features of the School of the Future characterize each of the four demonstration sites: (1) the integration of a broad spectrum of health and human services in public schools; (2) involvement of parents and teachers in the program activities; (3) involvement of many organizations, both public and private, as partners; (4) a strong commitment to the project by superintendents, principals, and other school administrators; and (5) a willingness to participate in the evaluation of the project.

Three levels of child development are targeted at each demonstration site: preschool, elementary school (grades K–5), and middle school (grades 6–8). At each level many approaches are being integrated in a comprehensive program of health and human services, with the particular combination of services dependent upon local needs and resources. At the preschool level examples of potential services include Head Start, Parents as Teachers, primary health care, and programs for siblings of children already in school. At elementary and middle schools services will focus upon the treatment or prevention of a variety of mental health problems, such as substance abuse, child abuse, school dropouts, teen pregnancy, and suicide, as well as on enrichment programs to promote self-esteem, effective interpersonal relations, and sound human development.

The overarching goal of the School of the Future project is to enrich and enhance the lives of children in these four communities. Education, physical health, and mental health are all expected to be positively impacted by the project over time. To accomplish this goal, the development of a long-term collaboration between local human service agencies, public school systems, and communities of teachers and parents must also be an emphasis of the project. At least five objectives are associated with this goal. Some will be given a higher priority than others, and many may take several years to be realized. The following are some of the objectives that the various sites and the Hogg Foundation are determined to accomplish within the next five years:

1. To improve the social and academic performance of students by involving their parents and the community in their education.
2. To identify and build upon the strengths of children, families, schools, and the community.
3. To offer enrichment programs that promote self-esteem and positive human development.
4. To coordinate services for children and their families in their own neighborhood.
5. To prevent or treat a variety of problems such as substance abuse, child abuse, school dropout, teen pregnancy, and suicide.

Each school develops programs and activities to meet the special needs of students and families. Parent involvement, for example, can take many forms. In San Antonio, a Parent Volunteer Corps has been created to help in the classrooms. In Austin, parents are involved in a Community Advisory Committee that organized a mental health information fair on the school site. In Houston, parent groups provide valuable information on the needs of community children. In Dallas, a Parents Advisory Committee has been formed to assist in developing programs.

Each of the four sites has an experienced social worker as project coordinator. Responsibilities of the coordinator include the following:

1. Working with school administrators and teachers.
2. Establishing links among school district personnel, local agencies, and other potential resources for the school's children and their families.
3. Developing parent education, job training, and support programs that encourage parents to become involved.
4. Identifying major concerns and needs of the students and their families.
5. Creating an awareness of the program among school personnel, members of the community, and people who provide services and funding.

Each of the schools is located in a predominantly low-income, minority neighborhood. In Austin, slightly less than 50 percent of the students in the project's elementary and middle schools are Hispanic, about 25 percent African-American, and the remaining 25 percent Anglo. The two elementary and one middle school for Houston are located in a very poor, predominantly Hispanic neighborhood but with a significant number of African-Americans. San Antonio's project is in a west side heavily Hispanic neighborhood that contains the oldest public housing project in the country. The two elementary schools in Dallas are located in a former shopping center that has been converted into a school facility with many interesting features from the point of view of human services, recreation, and mental health services. Together with the nearby middle school, this multipurpose facility serves a predominantly poor, African-American neighborhood.

Initiation of the four projects has unleashed a wide array of resources and activities that local school personnel, human service providers, and social agencies were ready to offer. Local leaders were both greatly stimulated and relieved to learn that the Foundation would support each School of the Future for at least five years and perhaps as many as ten or fifteen, depending upon the progress made, the significance of the outcome, and the need for continued support. Long-range planning with the involvement of many partners at each site meant stability and reassurance that careful initial planning would pay off dividends in the long run. There is no external monitor insisting upon immediate implementation or quick results, thus allowing each site to proceed deliberately at its own pace. It may well take two or three years before all of the components visualized as important for the School of the Future are properly in place.

A finely tuned balance has been achieved between the four local sites and the centralized activities for which the Hogg Foundation staff and its advisers are assuming responsibility. Every effort has been made to encourage each site to develop its own detailed plans and procedures within the overall guidelines. Representatives of the major stakeholders at each site have their own governance mechanisms that include school personnel, parents, human service agencies, and others. All the professional staff of the Foundation participate actively in various policy and planning activities of a centralized nature. Senior staff members of the Foundation serve as liaison consultants to each of the four sites. Periodic meetings of key personnel from the Foundation, from The University of Texas, and from each of the experimental programs help to maintain good communications. Funds from the Foundation are provided for occasional conferences among the four coordinators, as well as frequent visits to exchange ideas. An informal newsletter is distributed to more than 100 active participants.

Research and Evaluation

An essential feature of the Foundation's School of the Future is the plan to undertake research and evaluation at each of the four sites. The major long-term investment of resources and the opportunity for longitudinal follow-up of thousands of children and their families present a unique opportunity to conduct significant kinds of research and evaluation on which future policy decisions can be based. Provision has been made for a small number of specific research projects as proposed by qualified specialists, so long as the projects enrich the overall plans rather than detracting from them. Several such projects are already under way at each site.

Results of the evaluation will provide individuals and agencies with information on how to start a school-based service program and will offer key decision-makers reliable information on which to base future policies. Moreover, the assessment and follow-up of thousands of children and their cohorts in the four sites over many years will yield a unique set of scientifically valuable data on child development, educational practices, school organizations, community attitudes and behavior, and family development. For these reasons, special efforts were made right from the beginning by the Foundation and its advisers to deal with a number of critical questions relating to the evaluation design and its implementation.

A full-time behavioral scientist within the Hogg Foundation serves as director of evaluation. Five doctoral candidates in psychology, sociology, and social work help with data collection and analysis under the director's supervision. A group of evaluation experts comprised of University of Texas faculty members and key advisers in each of the four cities meets regularly to discuss technical issues and offer advice on methods for handling difficult evaluation questions. Special efforts have been made during the past few months to ensure that adequate baseline data will be obtained for as many children as possible at each of the four sites before major installation of new programs and restructuring of the schools that will constitute the School of the Future. In addition, comparable data will be obtained from other similar schools within each of the four cities to serve as comparison or control cases for the longitudinal study of change in subsequent years.

Future Prospects

As the School of the Future evolves in the next several years, vigorous efforts and skillful leadership will be necessary to achieve the goals that have been established. Additional partners will have to be drawn into the project, both to provide stronger financial support and to ensure the needed involvement of other community organizations and leaders, as well as the parents and other local citizens within the neighborhoods surrounding the demonstration sites.

While it is too early to say how permanent these four experimental programs will be, it is already clear that each of them has set long-range objectives and intends to continue in an experimental mode for years to come. The publicized, long-term commitment of the Foundation has been particularly valuable in encouraging all participants to be creative, flexible, and farsighted in their vision of what they want the School of the Future to become.

Psychologists and other behavioral scientists associated with the project have likewise been greatly stimulated to think of ways in which they can make a valuable contribution to education by taking part in the School of the Future program. Faculty and graduate students within several universities are already developing plans to take advantage of these settings for the advanced training of students and the conduct of relevant research.

It is important to keep in mind that the long-range goal of the School of the Future concept is to improve the conditions of teaching and learning within public schools by addressing the fundamental personal and social problems that currently interfere with such learning for many children and their families. Providing the necessary family and social support essential for sound child development and improving the school climate within which learning takes place are fundamental goals that must be achieved if our society is to meet the challenges ahead of us in the next century.

Fortunately, the country is awakening to the need for such reform, as evidenced by the new legislation proposed in Congress and the new efforts on the part of the president and executive branch to address these issues. What form these national programs will take is still unclear, but there is no longer any doubt major reforms will be launched by new public and private initiatives.

References

Comer, J. P. (1980). *School power.* New York: Free Press.

Comer, J. P. (1988). Educating poor minority children. *Scientific American, 259,* 42–48.

Guernsey, B. P. (1990). *Denver school-based clinics: A community partnership for youth.* Princeton, NJ: Robert Wood Johnson Foundation.

Haynes, N. M., Comer, J. P., & Hamilton-Lee, M. (1988). The school development program: A model for school improvement. *Journal of Negro Education, 57,* 11–21.

Johnson, D. L., & Breckenridge, J. N. (1982). The Houston Parent-Child Development Center and primary prevention of behavior problems in young children. *American Journal of Community Psychology, 10,* 305–316.

Kirst, M.W., McLaughlin, M., & Massell, D. (1990). Rethinking children's policy: Implications for educational administration. In B. Mitchell & L. Cunningham (Eds.), *National Society for the Study of Education yearbook: 1989: Pt. 2. Educational leadership and changing contexts of families, communities, and schools.* Chicago: National Society for the Study of Education.

Meyerhoff, M. K., & White, B. L. (1986, November). New parents as teachers. *Educational Leadership,* pp. 42–46.

Palaich, R.M., Whitney, T. N., & Paolino, A. R. (1991). *Changing delivery systems: Addressing the fragmentation in children and youth services.* Denver: Education Commission of the States.

Perry, N. J. (1989, December 4). How to help America's schools. *Fortune,* pp. 137–142.

Porter, P. J. (1990). *Access to comprehensive school-based health services for adolescents.* Brookline, MA: Harvard University School-Based Adolescent Health Care Program.

Zigler, E. F. (1989). Addressing the nation's child care crisis: The School of the 21st Century. *American Journal of Orthopsychiatry, 59,* 485–491.

Zigler, E. F., & Lang, M. E. (1991). *Child care choices.* New York: Free Press.

CHAPTER 2

Process Evaluation: Exploring the Realities Behind Education and Social Service Reforms

by

Rosemary Ellmer & Laura Lein

The Research Problem

At the most abstract level, the purpose of this research project is to explore and document the sociological, political, and organizational realities that underlie the process of education and social service reforms in urban areas. The process assessment studies the costs and benefits to children, families, and schools of projects like the School of the Future. In so doing, the assessment explores the experiences of all individuals participating in and contributing to the program. This process evaluation is characterized by an ethnographic research approach. Thus, the study will explore the meaning and process of organizational change from the perspective of participants at all levels. It identifies and documents the barriers to successful implementation of the School of the Future program and the conditions for its success. Within this framework, however, the conceptualization and goals of the process evaluation of the School of the Future Project are multifaceted:

- The record produced by the research project will provide documentation to assist with future understanding and dissemination of information about the project.
- Another purpose of the process evaluation is to provide ongoing feedback to the project while in progress. The process evaluation will serve the function of a formative evaluation by assisting the project directors to better achieve their goals through ongoing feedback of important qualitative information as it unfolds.
- Information obtained from a historical and socioanthropological data collection method will also enrich the findings of the more formal outcome evaluation efforts of the School of the Future project. For example, descriptive information about differences

in demographic, bureaucratic, program conception, or staffing patterns among sites could help explain programmatic or outcome measure differences that are expected to emerge.

- The process evaluation will provide policymakers and planners with a detailed account of the implementation of an innovative education and social services program. Such documentation will enhance the possibilities for replication of the School of the Future project. For instance, it is not difficult to achieve a consensus that interagency collaboration should occur and even that schools may well be the natural site for the concentration of integrated social service delivery efforts. However, there is often a gap between the conviction that things "ought" to happen and the reality of whether they actually can or do happen. The process evaluation will define critical issues and problem areas requiring attention at each phase of the project's development.
- The process evaluation will contribute to the general field of evaluation and assessment. There is a strong need for research methodologies to evaluate the efficiency and impact of "packages" of social services requiring interagency collaboration and coordination. Recent research indicates the importance of providing families with better-organized and more tailored services. Such service packages can draw on agencies ranging from the school to community to large publicly funded social service agencies. A fuller qualitative description and understanding of the development and implementation of a multiagency effort can enhance knowledge concerning the most useful ways to evaluate such projects.

Background to the Problem

Several bodies of available theory, data, and methodology are relevant to the argument underlying this research. These include (1) assessments of risk factors for children, (2) ethnographic studies of the persistently poor, (3) school and education ethnographic studies, and (4) studies concerning the role of schools in early intervention. A brief overview of these areas is presented, as each applies to the proposed research.

Risk Factors for Children. There is increasing evidence that certain children are at risk for specific emotional disorders. The nationally established prevalence rate for emotional disturbance among youth is 11.8 percent. An estimated 20 percent of children from families whose income is

below poverty level may suffer from a mental disorder or emotional disturbance (Gould, Wunsch-Hitzig, & Dohrewend, 1981). Thus, it becomes
increasingly important to identify such children early in an effort to prevent
or reduce the effects of disability. Some of the most severe environmental risk
factors associated with higher rates of mental health problems in children are
poverty, minority ethnic status, parental psychopathology, physical or other
maltreatment, a teenage parent, premature birth, low birth weight, parental
divorce, and serious childhood illness (Tuma, 1989).

These environmental risk factors rarely occur in isolation; more
common is the occurrence of several risk factors together, often in the
context of a broad risk factor such as low socioeconomic status. Currently, an
estimated one-third of all homeless Americans are members of families with
children (National Academy of Sciences, Institute of Medicine, 1989; Johnson, Sum, & Weill, 1989).

Other factors influencing a child's development are parental attitudes toward child rearing and quality of parent-child interactions, as well as
the child's intellectual activities, motivations, personality, and achievements.
These risk factors can negatively affect the accomplishment of important
developmental tasks such as the development of significant peer relationships and autonomy in adolescence (Tuma, 1989).

Approximately 1.2 to 1.5 million children and adolescents, ages 10
through 17, run away from home each year in the United States. Among these
youth, many are victims of abuse and neglect, some have had negative
experiences in foster care, and others have serious emotional problems for
which they receive no help. Upward of one-third are running from physical
or sexual abuse and 40 percent from other family problems such as parental
alcoholism or marital conflict. Additionally, many juveniles involved in the
judicial system have histories of abuse and neglect or serious emotional
disturbance. These youth are also significantly behind their peers in academic skills. Furthermore, poor children, regardless of race, are three times
more likely than affluent children to drop out of school. Poverty has been
deemed a key predictor of school dropout (National Academy of Sciences,
Institute of Medicine, 1989; Johnson, Sum, & Weill, 1989).

Ethnographic Studies of the Persistently Poor. The ordinarily piecemeal approach to the provision of human services has a number of implications for families in persistent poverty. First, individuals in persistently poor
communities may be eligible for multiple services, even within the same
human needs area. In few settings does a single service meet a household's
needs, even in one particular need domain (e.g., food, medical care,

housing). In some domains, individuals do, and are allowed to, take advantage of multiple programs, each with different regulations, eligibility criteria, and benefits. In other domains, the single most advantageous program must be selected. They operate with constraints which prohibit receipt of overlapping services (Lein, 1991).

Rachel and Her Children by Kozol (1988) was an ethnographically based examination of the homeless in New York City. Here we see the difficulties in negotiating the welfare environment. Kozol made a strong argument for the irrationality of the current welfare establishment, and its financial and human inefficiency in helping the homeless. Furthermore, in this work we see the power of a more ethnographic methodology in eliciting the relatively invisible experiences of a public service clientele.

Because of the large number of varied programs, individuals in persistently poor communities are likely to receive a "package" of services from a wide variety of sources (Lein, 1991). This occurs for at least two fundamental reasons. First, few services, taken alone, adequately respond to household needs. Second, even within a specific domain of need, regulations limit what a household may acquire. Specific services may be incapable of meeting even basic family needs. Corrected for inflation, the purchasing power of major cash transfer programs has remained about the same over the past twenty years (Palmer & Sawhill, 1982). For most federal programs there remain substantial differences in payments within and among regions of the country (Levitan, 1985). Therefore, members of persistently poor families consistently interact with many agencies in order to provide for household needs in any one domain, such as education, nutrition, or health care.

At a recent conference on "Models of Underclass Behavior" co-sponsored by the Joint Center for Political Studies and the U.S. Department of Health and Human Services (March 7–8, 1990, Washington, D.C.) there was continuing discussion of the need for a more ethnographic and contextual approach to understanding the behavior and decision making among persistently poor families and individuals and their relationships with the institutions serving them.

School and Education Ethnographies

Schools, in particular, have proven to be exceptional laboratories in which to trace children's reactions to institutional and organizational environments. Schools are providing increasing numbers of social services. For most students, teachers represent the values and traditions of the mainstream society. Research beginning with Cazden (1972) and Philips (1982) has explored the significance of class and cultural differences between children and the staff and faculty of schools from the perspective of the children and their parents.

This kind of research has boomed lately with such edited volumes as "Explaining the School Performance of Minority Students" (Jacob & Jordan, 1987). In this volume a selection of articles examines the impact of schools on more general social change. In particular, they explore the impact of multiple innovations on a range of ethnic minorities.

Studies Concerning the Role of Schools in Early Intervention. The rationale for early identification and intervention services is supported by the findings of Stroul and Friedman (1986). They contended that intervention occurring at the point of identification of a problem can impact the duration and severity of the problem, as well as reduce the overall prevalence of disturbance in children.

As children become of school age, the school becomes the logical place to identify those who are beginning to show signs of emotional, behavioral, health, and academic problems. It is also the logical point of intervention. For many minority families the school becomes the central focus in the community because it has played a major role in adding cohesion to families and the neighborhood. Early interventions that are school based can provide training, counseling, support, and linkage with other services. Such efforts at early identification and intervention at school sites necessitate close relationships with other systems of service delivery (Stroul & Friedman, 1986).

As a major institution, the school can be the beginning point of collaboration with other agencies. Interagency collaboration has received particular attention during the past ten years as a process through which community resources can be combined. The scope of this concept and its use have broadened considerably under the economic mandates and constraints of the late 1970s, leading to a search for the best way to use a variety of resources at the smallest cost in the provision of services to youth. Johnson and McLaughlin (1982) found that the coordination of service delivery systems has an economic benefit while also providing services based on a continuum of child needs across social, psychological, medical, vocational, and educational domains.

Research Methodology

The ethnographic approach is designed to illuminate the categories by which program participants conceptualize the institutional change process and the patterns which typify that process. The process evaluation of the School of the Future project responds to the need for qualitative research on issues related to persistent poverty and the underclass. The qualitative data analysis techniques employed by the researchers have been described by Miles and Huberman (1984). These techniques represent a systematic method for cataloging, interpreting, and presenting the results of qualitative research. Qualitative materials are first sorted by topic area and then by specific themes within the topic area. Pattern searches are made to elicit the constellations of attitudes held by groups within the study population. The triangulation of multiple approaches (interviews of different individuals in different settings by different researchers) insures that the findings are not the artifact of one particular subset of the data. In addition to a review and analysis of all records and correspondence related to the project, the researchers are conducting in-depth interviews with persons identified as pivotal to the development or evaluation of the project. Observational techniques are also being employed in the various project settings.

Basic Research Instrument. After conducting initial reviews of Hogg Foundation records and completing a set of pilot interviews, the research team developed a detailed schema to guide the data collection for the process evaluation. The schema (presented in Appendix 1) divides the history of the School of the Future project into four phases: development, adoption, implementation, and institutionalization. A detailed account of each site's history will be based on interviews with participants at the Hogg Foundation, in the school district offices, in the schools, and in the School of the Future program.

The interviews themselves are designed to elicit from the interviewees a detailed chronology of project events as experienced by that individual. A critical incident approach will allow for the systematic collection of detailed accounts of incidents that characterize the project for the individual. Such accounts of incidents are particularly amenable to pattern analysis as proposed by Miles and Huberman (1984). Due to the complexity of the School of the Future project, a number of participants will be interviewed at the Hogg Foundation and in each site.

At each school site, researchers are interviewing, at a minimum, the principal, school counselors, the site coordinator, other site staff, the school nurse, members of the advisory group to the project, active parent volunteers, and selected teachers. Furthermore, the researchers are completing interviews with the central school administration liaison with oversight responsibilities, as well as associated Hogg Foundation staff and other technical advisors. Where the site has drawn on the resources of other community organizations and programs, researchers are interviewing representatives of those programs.

The schedule for interviewing each key informant varies according to the depth of that individual's involvement and schedule. In order to accommodate the complexity of the interviewing process, multiday visits are planned to each site on a monthly basis. An open-ended interview schedule has been developed that is adaptable to both the level of involvement of the key informant (i.e., school administrator, project coordinator, service provider, etc.) and the level of the project development (i.e., development, adoption, implementation, or institutionalization phase). Two examples of the interview schedule applicable to different respondents and different levels of the project's development are presented in Appendix 2. Due to the ethnographic approach, the questions in the interview protocol represent an outline for structuring the interview rather than a formal script. Within each interview, a critical incident approach is taken, asking for specific illustrative examples of each point in significant detail.

With information gathered according to such an interview outline and from an extensive list of key informants, it will be possible to develop comparative site profiles from the four quite diverse sites. The use of extended interviews with a range of respondents permits us to impose a systematic method on the data collection process, while still allowing the collection of material documenting the idiosyncratic variations from one site to another. Furthermore, the interview material is subjected to content analysis for themes and patterns that transcend individual site variability.

Discussion

By the end of 1991 the research team had completed eight months of data collection on the process evaluation component of the School of the Future project. Although, of course, it is far too early in the research process to offer conclusions with any confidence, certain themes already have emerged with unmistakable clarity. The following, while tentative, are a few examples of the kind of data and eventual analysis we have already begun to develop:

- Some early comments from respondents are useful as immediate and formative feedback to the School of the Future. For instance, in the course of interviews, the four site coordinators pressed for more opportunities for informal contact just among themselves. Although site coordinators have met together on a regular basis, such meetings have usually occurred in the context of larger groups that include school administrators, evaluation staff, and consultants at the Hogg Foundation.

- Administrative differences among the sites promise to have far-reaching effects. Site coordinators vary in the amount of time allotted to their position, in their positioning in the school system hierarchy, and in their job descriptions. Sites vary according to the formal recipient of funding—the school or another agency. Sites vary in the degree of project monitoring by the district-level school administration.

- These specific kinds of administrative differences are reflected in broader variations among the sites. It is clear that the school systems in each city offer schools and principals widely divergent degrees of autonomy. The degree of autonomy appears to have considerable significance in determining perceived ownership of and commitment to the project.

- Project staff perceive the initial grant as too small to accomplish the goals of the program, as anticipated by the Hogg Foundation. Each site has sought additional resources. The methods for seeking different resources and the degree of success vary considerably among the sites.

- Site personnel are considerably puzzled by the evaluation process. Each site has site-specific notions concerning the evaluation, the appropriate role of the Hogg Foundation, and the degree to which outsiders to the school should participate in the evaluation.

At this point, these preliminary findings are all merely suggestive. However, as the process assessment continues, we expect to formalize these, and a number of other findings, pertinent to the replication of major programs such as the School of the Future. These findings will be presented in several ways. The expected products of this research will include analysis and interpretation of the factors within each phase that have an impact on later phases. In more general terms, the main products of the proposed project will include the following:

1. A historical record detailing significant factors pertaining to each of the four phases outlined above
2. A detailed analysis of the political and social process underlying institutional innovation, drawing on four diverse sites
3. A developed research schema to allow for ongoing record keeping across sites on a standardized basis.

We perceive the School of the Future project as a particularly exciting, innovative program. This detailed assessment of its implementation and development should provide useful information for others who wish to implement experimental programs elsewhere.

Appendix 1
Data Collection Guide

I. **Developmental phase**
   A. Hogg Foundation (internal work)
      1. History and origin of the concept
      2. Initial groundwork and internal considerations
      3. Development of the idea into concept paper
      4. Development of criteria for site selection
   B. Hogg Foundation (external work)
      1. First contacts with school district and relevant community leaders
      2. Invitations to submit proposals from particular sites

II. **Adoption phase**
   A. Site response to request for proposal
      1. Necessary agreements and assurances
      2. Bureaucratic considerations
      3. Development of team to write proposal
   B. Definition of parties and players
      1. Initial involvement of parents and community representatives
      2. Selection of particular schools
      3. Initial involvement of school principals and other school personnel

III **Implementation phase**
   A. Development of bureaucratic and logistical components
      1. Location and space
         a. Quantity and quality of space
         b. Responsibility for any necessary renovations
      2. Development of bureaucratic structure
         a. Lines of control and reporting
         b. Development of process of multigroup participation
         c. Development of advisory and other controlling groups
      3. Budget process
         a. Budgetary control
         b. Sources of support
      4. Selection of site director
         a. Internal or general search
         b. School/community involvement
   B. Development of service components
      1. Design and implementation of plan for service components
      2. Solicitation of service agencies for cooperation
         a. Kinds of agencies and programs

    b. Review and decisions concerning participating agencies

   3. Development of contracts and other relationships

    a. Informal or formal contracts

    b. Control over access to school

  C. Development of evaluation components

   1. Assignment of advisers, consultants, and research assistants

    a. Hogg Foundation involvement

    b. Site involvement

   2. Definition of evaluation goals and methods:

    a. Hogg Foundation involvement

     (1) Plans for cross-site evaluation

     (2) Review of site proposals for evaluation

    b. Site involvement

   3. Determination of intra- and inter-site data needs and evaluation

IV. **Institutionalization phase**

  A. Monitoring of staffing, service, bureaucratic, logistical, and evaluation components

   1. Documentation of proposal implementation, including alterations, changes in priorities

   2. Personnel issues and concerns

   3. Bureaucratic issues and concerns

  B. Impediments to project's progress

  C. Influences of site variability on program development, goals, and outcomes

  D. Continuing development of evaluation process

Appendix 2
Examples of Interview Protocols

Example 1:

Level of Involvement of Key Informant: School principal

Level of Project Development: First contact with School of the Future

1. Could you tell us about the first time you heard about the School of the Future project?

  Probes: Who first mentioned the idea to you?

    When and in what setting did you hear of this idea?

2. What were your initial reactions to the program?

  Probes: Were you able to discuss these with others?

    Did you feel responsible for solving any problems?

3. What were some of the initial concerns (economic, political, social/cultural, etc.) you had regarding the program as you understood it at the time?

  Probes: Give me an example of one issue that arose for you.

    How did this issue emerge?

    What eventually happened?

    What is another issue? etc.

4. What, if any, were some of the most pressing needs in the school and community that you saw could be addressed by the project?

Probes: Give me an example from the last week or two.
What kind of need arose?
Can the School of the Future address that need?

5. At what point did you understand that you would be involved with the project?
   Probes: From whom did you learn about your involvement?
   What were you first expected to do?
   What were your first reactions to being involved?

Example 2:
Level of Involvement of Key Informant: Project coordinator
Level of Project Development: Planning phase

1. What did your involvement in the planning phase of the project first encompass?
   Probes: What activities did you engage in?
   What kinds of decisions did you have to make?
   To whom did you report?
   Did you supervise anyone else involved in the project?
   How were they selected?

2. Who were some of the principal participants you worked with in the planning phase of the project? What did they do?
   Probes: How did you first meet some of these individuals?
   What was your first reaction to working with them?
   How were the responsibilities divided?

3. What were some of the groups involved in the planning stage of the project?
   Probes: Why did each group join in?
   How did you learn about each group?
   Can you characterize your first interaction with each group?
   What was each group's contribution?

4. Were you aware of any major points of disagreement among involved parties that had to be resolved during this phase?
   Probes: Were you involved in formulating the solution?
   Were there any problems that have continued to drag on?

5. What were the major issues that needed to be addressed in the planning phase of a project like this?
   Probes: What did you see as the primary issue?
   To what degree were you responsible for finding the solution?
   How did you feel about the process by which issues were addressed?

6. What were the major difficulties you have experienced in the planning phase of this project?
   Probes: Can you give some examples of these difficulties?
   Can you describe how each one was addressed?

7.   What were the major successes you experienced in the planning phase of this project?
     Probes: Can you give some examples of these successes?
     Can you describe how each one emerged?

References

Cazden, C. (1972). *Functions of language in the classroom.* New York: Teachers College Press.

Gould, M., Wunsch-Hitzig, R., & Dohrewend, B. (1981). Estimating the prevalence of childhood psychopathology: A critical review. *Journal of the American Academy of Child Psychiatry, 20,* 462–476.

Jacob, E., & Jordan, C. (Eds.). (1987). Explaining the school performance of minority students. *Anthropology and Education Quarterly, 18* (4).

Johnson, C. M., Sum, A. M., & Weill, J. D. (1989). The economic plight of America's young families: An update of Children's Defense Fund's *Vanishing Dreams Report.* Washington, DC: Children's Defense Fund.

Johnson, J., & McLaughlin, R. (1982). Interagency collaboration: Driving and restraining forces. *Exceptional Children, 48*(5), 395–399.

Joint Center for Political Studies and Health and Human Services. (1990, March). *Models of underclass behavior.* Unpublished conference proceedings.

Kozol, J. (1988). *Rachel and her children.* New York: Fawcett Columbine.

Lein, L. (1991). The role of food programs in the lives of persistently poor children. Manuscript in preparation.

Levitan, S. (1985). *Programs in aid of the poor.* Baltimore: Johns Hopkins University Press.

Miles, M., & Huberman, M. (1984). *Qualitative data analysis.* Beverly Hills, CA: Sage.

National Academy of Sciences, Institute of Medicine. (1989). *Research on children and adolescents with mental, behavioral, and developmental disorders.* Washington, DC: National Academy Press.

Palmer, J., & Sawhill, I. (1982). *The Reagan experiment.* Washington, DC: Urban Institute Press.

Philips, S. (1982). *The invisible culture.* New York: Longman.

Stroul, B., & Friedman, R. (1986). *A system of care for severely emotionally disturbed children and youth.* Washington, DC: CAASP Technical Assistance Center.

Tuma, J. M. (1989). Mental health services for children: The state of the art. *American Psychologist, 44,* 188–199.

CHAPTER 3

Outcome Evaluation: Plans for a
Five-Year Longitudinal Study Across Sites

by

Ralph E. Culler & Scott S. Keir

The School of the Future has important implications for how public schools can be utilized effectively in the twenty-first century. Because of the national significance of the effort, a careful and thorough evaluation has been built into the program. Better student mental and physical health is the long-term goal of the School of the Future, but short-term improvements in school climate, school-community relations, and parental involvement are viewed as the necessary steps to reaching that goal. Measures of both short-term and long-term variables are included in the evaluation design. The results of the evaluation of the short-term objectives will help redirect the project in its formative stages, while the results from the long-term variables will show the effectiveness of the school-based approach in improving the quality of life for school children.

Purpose

The results of the evaluation will be used to

- *Assist in Site Planning.* After data are collected, appropriate information will be "filtered" back to the sites to help them in planning. Aggregated information provided to the sites will be useful in prioritizing programs that need to be developed and implemented in the school. Sites may also use the information to promote the school-based approach with local service providers.
- *Inform Key Decision-Makers.* Reliable research on the effectiveness of the school-based approach will be provided to legislators and other key stakeholders. By demonstrating the benefits of the School of the Future concept, local, state, or federal support may be garnered for trying the school-based approach in other schools.

- *Develop a Blueprint for Replication:* One of the objectives of the evaluation will be to document the successes and failures in each of the project sites. This documentation, combined with other important data, such as budget estimates, will provide valuable information to those interested in implementing school-based service projects in their communities.

Both ethnographic and quantitative techniques are being employed in the evaluation. Information will be collected from students, parents, teachers, counselors, school administrators, and key informants from the community. The research is currently planned for a five-year period, but may well continue into the twenty-first century.

Methodology

The evaluation for the School of the Future project was developed after investigating past and current efforts to evaluate school-based service projects (Center for Research in Human Development and Education, 1990; Peng, Agrawal, McLaughlin, Scannapieco, & Weishaw, 1991). The final design is a nonrandomized experimental/control group pre-post design. In each of the four sites, one middle school and one (or two) of its feeder elementary schools were selected as School of the Future sites. For evaluation design purposes, an equal number of schools in each site was identified as control or comparison schools. These schools were matched on demographic characteristics (student enrollment, ethnic breakdown, percent reduced/free lunch program) with the experimental schools. In three of the four sites, data have been collected from the comparison schools. The identification of comparison schools in one of the sites is still under discussion. Therefore, eventually there will be 21 schools (11 experimental and 10 comparison) actively participating in the School of the Future project evaluation.

The plan calls for an across-site comparison as well as a within-site comparison. Data collection procedures have been standardized as much as possible in the first year so that similarities and differences in outcomes can be analyzed across the sites. The evaluation staff will also be able to compare outcomes within sites between project and comparison schools. Some data will be obtained in the 1991–92 school year for nearly 12,000 children in the participating schools.

The data collected annually on students from the survey and the achievement data transferred from the school computer files will be matched with the project's data sets. Repeated assessment of the same students in

Table 1

Number of Students Participating in the
School of the Future Evaluation by Site and Grade Level

City	Grade	Program	Comparison	Total
Austin	K–5	972	558	1,530
	6–7	725	650	1,375
Dallas	K–5	600	600[a]	1,200
	6–7	400	400[a]	800
Houston	K–5	726	799	1,525
	6–7	710	679	1,389
San Antonio	K–5	1,648	855	2,503
	6–8	910	630	1,540
Totals	All grades and cities	6,691	5,171	11,862

[a] Incomplete, estimated

these sites and the comparison schools will be performed over at least a five-year period. Panel studies will be made of students (as long as they stay in the school district) from kindergarten through the eighth grade. These longitudinal studies will permit the measurement of change in specific cohorts of students over time. Path analysis of select groups will be possible to evaluate the impact of specific interventions (taking into account the influences produced by age, period, and cohort effects) (Glenn, 1977).

Cross-sectional analyses will also be made in the evaluation. By studying each grade level at one point in time, a better understanding can be gained of the differences between students' needs in the upper grades as opposed to the needs in the lower grades.

Data Collection

Key Informant Survey. A key informant survey has been administered to a sample of teachers, parents, administrators, and community leaders (approximately 20 hour-long interviews were conducted in each site). The survey gathers information about the school, neighborhood, and the existing strengths and weaknesses from individuals who were identified as being very knowledgeable about the school and community. The interviews were conducted by the project's graduate research associates, and subjects included all of the principals, counselors, and nurses, as well as a sample of the teachers and parents at each school. The purpose was to collect qualitative information on the school climate and school/community relationship before the School of the Future was in full operation. It also serves as a form of needs assessment that will be helpful to the sites in deciding which services should be a priority for the schools to develop and implement. The survey will be repeated on an annual basis at each site.

Preliminary results demonstrate that each site has its share of strengths along with areas that need improvement. Most respondents interviewed for this survey indicated that parents in the community were, in fact, interested in becoming involved in the school and their children's school activities, but for various reasons did not. Some indicated that parents did not know how they could help the school or felt uncomfortable in the school.

Those interviewed believed that there must be more outreach on the part of the school to get parents to come in and make them feel comfortable there. Suggestions included developing parent volunteer groups that use parents who are already involved as "recruiters," classes for parents that offer topics that they feel are important and relevant in helping to rear their children, opening the school after hours for the parents and their children for both recreation and classes, and providing transportation and child care for those who want to come to the school for activities.

Many respondents expressed concern about the lack of security in the neighborhoods. In fact, many said that this fear was one reason parents do not come to the schools very often. They are afraid to leave their homes unoccupied and unprotected from burglars.

One of the strengths noted by most of the respondents in the four sites was the high level of communication offered by the teachers in the elementary schools. Principals and teachers were commended for their dedication to the students at this grade level. Their willingness to concern themselves with issues outside of the classroom was perceived as a genuine resource in the community.

Respondents also said that each of these schools was doing a good job of attracting the private sector and business to become involved in the schools. This involvement varies from offering mentors for the students to making donations to the schools for the purchase of supplies and services.

Those surveyed believed the involvement of businesses is also having a positive effect on the entire community.

Despite the economic disadvantage present in each of the sites, optimism was expressed by the individuals interviewed in this survey. They were aware of the problems that exist in their community and saw the potential for the schools in their neighborhood to help improve the current situation. Yet their optimism is heavily tempered with caution. They have seen programs come and go with the end result being very little. They will only be convinced when they see improvement in community involvement, school climate, and eventually student achievement.

Student Survey. The quantitative aspects of the project's evaluation will center primarily on the data collected from the student survey and the information collected routinely by the schools. Three instruments comprise the student survey for collection of baseline data before the new programs are fully implemented. All are recognized nationally and have extensive normative information available (Witt, Heffer, & Pfeiffer, 1990). In some cases, only a subscale of the full instrument is used. The student survey measures contribute primarily to the long-term outcome analysis, but some items target short-term areas, such as school climate.

The instruments discussed below have been tested and deemed appropriate for students in grades six through eight. (A different approach is being taken for children in kindergarten through fifth grade, using a teacher report form.) All three instruments are administered during a single class period, the completion taking no longer than 50 minutes.

Achenbach's Youth Self-Report (YSR). Achenbach's Youth Self-Report version of the Child Behavior Checklist (Achenbach, 1991b) is the core instrument in the student survey. It measures students' mental and physical health, including aggressive behavior, popularity, depression, delinquent behavior, somatic complaints, thought disorders, and identity problems. There are 122 items in the YSR that take approximately 30 minutes to complete.

National Education Longitudinal Study (NELS). The National Education Longitudinal Study has been used extensively by the Center for Education Statistics of the U.S. Department of Education to survey students on various school issues (National Center for Education Statistics, 1988). The "School Life" section of the NELS is being used in the School of the Future student survey. This section measures how students feel about their school, their teachers, and their classmates and will provide information on the students' perception of school climate. There are 13 items that take approximately 10 minutes to complete.

Self-Perception Profile for Adolescents. A third instrument in the student survey is the Self-Perception Profile for Adolescents, also known as Harter's Perceived Competencies Scales (Harter, 1982, 1985). The three most relevant subscales of the instrument are being used—Scholastic Competence, Social Acceptance, and General Self-Worth. These short scales measure students' feelings about their ability in school, their social relationships, and general happiness in life. A total of 15 items takes no more than 10 minutes to complete.

Each teacher was assisted in the administration by one graduate research associate. The survey was administered in the fall of 1991 to all sixth- and seventh-grade students who agreed to participate at both experimental and comparison schools. Data collection for students in the eighth grade will begin in the fall of 1992.

Achenbach's Teacher Report Form (TRF). Another version of the Child Behavior Checklist offered by Achenbach (Achenbach, 1991a) has been developed to be filled out by teachers on their students. The teacher report form is used with children in kindergarten through fifth grade who would not be able to complete the self-report version. (The Harter subscales and the School Life section of the NELS are not appropriate for the younger children.) In the experimental and comparison sites, information from teachers will be collected early in 1992 on all children in these lower grades through the use of the TRF. Each form should take approximately 15 minutes to complete per student. Teachers will be compensated for their time in supplying the information.

Outcome Measures

The direct target of the School of the Future is the student. The ultimate goal of the project is to improve the quality of life for these youngsters. It is clear from earlier studies that changes at the student level do not occur quickly. Two different kinds of outcomes are expected, short-term and long-term.

Short Term. In the short term, changes will be examined in three areas. The first is *school climate*, the perception of the school by the students, teachers, administrators, and parents. Data being collected will answer questions such as

Do the students enjoy going to school?

Do they feel safe at school?

Do they receive encouragement and support at school?

Do the parents feel comfortable going to the school?

Do the teachers enjoy working at the school?

The second area is *parental involvement*. Information on parental involvement will be gathered from teachers and administrators as well as directly from the parents. The data collected will help to answer questions such as

Are the parents involved in a wide range of school activities?

Do parents assist their children with homework assignments?

Do parents attend evening classes offered at the school?

Do the teachers recognize and encourage a broader parent role in the school?

Does the principal encourage parental involvement?

The third area is *school/community relationship*, the perception of the school by the community, recognizing that students, parents, and staff are an integral part of the community. The surveys answer questions such as

Are the students proud of their school?

Do the teachers participate in community/neighborhood projects?

Do the parents respect the principal as a community leader?

Do local service providers perceive the school as open and collaborative?

Long Term. In the long term the focus is upon changes in the students themselves. There are three areas where measurable positive changes are anticipated several years from now. The first long-term area is *student mental health*. Questions to be explored include

What is the level of students' self-esteem?

Are students happy most of the time?

Do many students suffer from periods of depression?

Do students exhibit any behavior problems?

The second long-term area is *physical health*. Some questions to be explored include

Do students experience any aches or pains?

How many students are using or have used alcohol?

Do the students have access to medical help?

To what degree do students engage in risky behaviors?

The third long-term area is *academic achievement*. Information to be collected here includes

What are the students' grades?

How do the students perform on standardized tests?

Do students attend class regularly?

What is the dropout rate?

School District Data

A great deal of information on students will be collected from the four school districts' computer data sets. Demographic variables such as ethnicity and socioeconomic level are included along with academic measures such as grades, standardized test scores, and attendance. With assistance from the research and evaluation departments at each of the school districts, individual student-level data on more than 50 variables will be transferred to the Foundation's computer data files. Most variables are available in a format that has been standardized for all Texas schools. In addition to the student-level information, aggregate-level data on the schools and the district will also be collected. The district-level data will allow comparison between the School of the Future students and other students in the same school district.

Staff and Advisers

The evaluation is directed by a sociologist with extensive experience in the evaluation of social programs in the Texas mental health system. This full-time director is assisted by five half-time graduate research associates, each assigned to one of the four sites and one with responsibility for centralized data collection and analysis. All are doctoral students in psychology, educational psychology, or social work at The University of Texas at Austin. Several are former Fellows in the Hogg Foundation's Evaluation Research Fellowship program.

The evaluation team receives support and technical assistance from the Foundation's executive staff. In addition to the internal staffing at the Foundation, the evaluation team is advised by a group of four experts on the faculty of The University of Texas at Austin from the Departments of Psychology and Educational Psychology and from the School of Social Work. This faculty group has been and will continue to be heavily involved in the design and implementation of the project's evaluation.

The Hogg Foundation staff and the four faculty advisers comprise the central staffing for the evaluation. This team is augmented by an additional group of three local social scientists, one for each of the sites distant from Austin. Each of the site-based advisers is familiar with local issues and can act quickly to help with evaluation-oriented problems at the site.

The complete evaluation team of staff and advisers met frequently during the design phase of the evaluation and continues to meet every few months to review the progress and redirect the effort where necessary. A separate research group is handling a qualitative analysis of the School of the Future from a historical perspective, covering the first 18 months of the project (see chapter 2).

Other Research Projects

Additional data are being gathered at some of the sites through other research efforts, as reported in subsequent chapters dealing with each of the four sites. The intent is to share information with qualified investigators and to incorporate relevant data from other research projects in the same schools and communities. For example, a risk behavior survey was administered in an independent project during spring 1991 at the Houston site. The goal of the survey was to determine whether or not the students in the Houston site exhibit risky behaviors as compared to other students surveyed across the country.

Among other research projects likely to develop at the project sites is one that will explore the effect of proximity to drugs and drug use on children's health and education. Another project will investigate how some children "beat the odds." Despite growing up in economically disadvantaged neighborhoods and sometimes coming from dysfunctional families, some children are still performing very well academically. This separate study will attempt to uncover the reasons why these children are overcoming the tremendous barriers to success and performing well in school.

Evaluation Problems and Issues

Although the evaluation of the School of the Future is just getting started, several problems have been encountered or anticipated. After much discussion with advisers and site personnel, some solutions have been provided, but there are still many hurdles to overcome as the project continues.

Different Expectations Regarding the Evaluation. Differences among the sites was expected to result in numerous difficulties for the evaluation. One of these differences that has been especially difficult to deal with has been in philosophy. In Dallas, for example, an approach was taken that emphasizes strengths rather than problems or weaknesses. The result has been a great deal of debate regarding the appropriateness of the survey instruments that are being used in the other three sites. The project leaders in Dallas decided that the use of Achenbach's Child Behavior Checklist, in either the student or teacher versions, was too problem-focused and not the best choice considering the political climate in that community. Dallas will be developing its own evaluation plan incorporating the self-concept and school climate survey instruments, as well as the standard districtwide data, but not including the Achenbach surveys. As a result, for many areas of the study the ability to compare students in this site to students in the other three sites will not be possible.

Student Mobility. Another anticipated problem is attrition in the schools over time. In the types of neighborhoods where the project schools are located, there is a great deal of mobility, resulting in a turnover of many students each year. Mobility rates run as high as 50 percent at some schools. Because of the likelihood that a significant portion of the original sample will be lost, data are being collected from the entire population of students in both experimental and control schools. Even if attrition is high in later years, the number of students participating in the evaluation should be satisfactory. Special efforts will be made to determine what biases, if any, result from selective attrition.

Parental Consent. The issue of informed consent for administering the survey to students was another issue which generated much discussion. All of the sites considered parental consent important, but some were interested in using an "active" consent procedure while others wanted a "passive" consent procedure. Active consent is a procedure asking a parent to sign and return the consent form in order to allow the child's participation in the study. Passive consent asks the parent to sign and return the form only if the parent does not want his or her child to participate. The disadvantage of active consent is the possible low rate of return of the consent forms, resulting in a lower student participation rate than would be ideal. The disadvantage of the passive procedure is the possibility that a parent who would disapprove of a child's participation may never receive the consent form.

In order to compensate for the disadvantages of passive consent, two of the schools using this procedure decided to mail home consent forms rather than send the forms home with the students. This reassured the school staff that parents received the forms and that when the forms were not returned, this nonresponse truly signified that the parents did not object to their children's participation in the survey.

Active consent did result in a very low return rate. In fact, two schools that initially chose active consent over passive consent changed the procedure by organizing a last minute mailout of passive consent forms because the return rate for active consent was so low. The principals of these two schools decided that even with the financial incentives created to increase the number of returned forms per class (money awarded to each class returning over 90 percent of the forms), not enough response was generated. The change in consent procedures resulted in a much larger participation rate for students in these schools.

Comparison Schools. Adding comparison schools to the study created several problems. First, it doubled the amount of data collection and related activities. Second, it has been difficult to find sets of schools which are identical in size and demographic composition and which also have the feeder relationship that is essential for following the students in the future. Third is the problem of obtaining entrée and cooperation from schools that are not receiving any of the benefits of the program.

Despite these difficulties, three of the four sites currently have identified comparison schools. It was stressed to the principals in those schools that there were benefits for their students and teachers who participate in the survey. The Foundation offered to provide the principals and staff with school summaries of their students based on the results of the student and teacher surveys. These reports will give the principals a better understanding of the needs of their students and may be valuable for planning in the coming years.

In addition, cash payments are being offered to all teachers of grades K–5 who complete teacher report forms, and small cash awards are provided to sixth- and seventh-grade classrooms for participation in the student surveys. These financial incentives also had a positive influence on the comparison schools' decision to take part in the evaluation.

Differences in Sites. Differences among the sites may complicate the data analysis if the data are analyzed in the aggregate. Each of the School of the Future sites is similar in that they are all located in neighborhoods with many problems and few resources. However, the sites differ in many ways. Two are predominantly Hispanic, one is African-American, and one is tri-ethnic. One neighborhood is much more impoverished than the others. In three of the sites, the project coordinator was hired by the school district; in the fourth by a private family service agency working in partnership with the schools.

There were also differences in the way the surveys were administered in each site. In order to gain the trust of the school staff, the evaluation staff had to be flexible. This often meant allowing the principals and staff to choose when and even how the administration of the survey would take place.

As a result, most of the administrations were performed in a small classroom setting, while one was conducted in a large hall with over 150 students. Also, some surveys were administered by evaluation staff while in many cases teachers were trained in the use of the instrument which they administered.

In the coming year, after some analyses are performed on the data collected, decisions will have to be made as to the best form of survey administration for the coming year. An effort will be made to standardize the administration process across the four sites based on the results of the preliminary data analyses.

Multisite projects often pose difficulties in program development and evaluation. While inter-site differences in needs, philosophies, and survey administration types can be a problem in assessing effectiveness of a project, these differences can also be viewed as important information. That is, multisite differences allow for "adaptations to local circumstances" and the ability to "detect and examine contextual effects" (Mowbray & Herman, 1991). Over time, the evaluation of the project should be able to address what works in one site as compared with what works in another, important information for any future application of what is learned.

References

Achenbach, T. M. (1991a). *Manual for the Teacher's Report Form and 1991 Profile*. Burlington: University of Vermont Department of Psychiatry.

Achenbach, T. M. (1991b). *Manual for the Youth Self-Report and 1991 Profile*. Burlington: University of Vermont Department of Psychiatry.

Center for Research in Human Development and Education. (1990). *Center for Education in the Inner Cities: A technical proposal*. Unpublished manuscript. Temple University, Philadelphia.

Glenn, N. D. (1977). *Cohort analysis*. Sage University Paper Series on Quantitative Applications in the Social Sciences, 07-001. Beverly Hills, CA: Sage.

Harter, S. (1982). The Perceived Competence Scale for Children. *Child Development, 53*, 87–97.

Harter, S. (1985). *Manual for the Self-Perception Profile for Children: Revision of the Perceived Competence Scale for Children*. Denver: University of Denver Department of Developmental Psychology.

Mowbray, C.T., & Herman, S.E. (1991). Using multiple sites in mental health evaluations: Focus on program theory and implementation issues. In R. S. Turpin & J. M. Sinacore (Eds.), *Multisite evaluations* (pp. 45–58). San Francisco: Jossey-Bass.

National Center for Education Statistics. (1988). *National Education Longitudinal Study of 1988*. Washington, DC: U.S. Department of Education.

Peng, S. S., Agrawal, A., McLaughlin, J., Scannapieco, M., & Weishaw, N. (1991). *Building an integrated data system for CEIC.* Unpublished paper. Temple University, Center for Research in Human Development and Education, Philadelphia.

Witt, J. C., Heffer, R. W., & Pfeiffer, J. (1990). Structured rating scales: A review of self-report and informant rating, processes, procedures, and issues. In C. R. Reynolds & R. W. Kamphaus (Eds.), *Handbook of psychological and educational assessment of children* (pp. 364–394). New York: Guilford.

CHAPTER 4

Paving the Way: Questions and Criteria for the School of the Future

by

Matia Finn-Stevenson

Educators, mental health professionals, and policymakers, among others, have called for major changes in the school, acknowledging the academic failure of many of our nation's children, specifically those from low-income families. One outcome of this focus on the education of low-income children has been the development of numerous school reform initiatives. The School of the Future is one of the latest such initiatives. Unlike other school reform programs which are more limited in their scope, the School of the Future represents an attempt to provide a comprehensive range of services from birth through adolescence, with the school serving as the locus for the delivery of such services.

There are other unique aspects to the program, not the least of these being the fact that its development is being fostered by researchers from the Hogg Foundation who are working in conjunction with educators in four Texas schools where the program is being implemented. The comprehensive nature of the School of the Future and the partnership between research and educational practice that it embodies make this a significant effort which may well pave the way for changes in the way we operate schools.

Since the School of the Future is still in a developmental phase, it would be useful to take a close look at how it is being implemented and evaluated. It would also be instructive to examine the School of the Future in the context of other programs for children and families and to look at the similarities, and differences, between these and the School of the Future.

Background: The National Scene

The School of the Future is built upon and draws from the conceptual basis of several programs that have been developed in the past one or two decades. Some of these programs seek to create changes in the organizational structure and climate of the school (e.g., Comer, 1991) or in the curriculum and teaching methodology (e.g., Slavin, Madden, Karweit, Livermon, & Lawrence, 1990) as the means of addressing the needs of low-income children and ensuring their academic success. Other school reform initiatives emphasize the importance of early intervention, calling for schools to provide early childhood education for low-income children beginning at age three or four (Committee for Economic Development, 1987). Impressed with the documented success of such programs as Head Start and the Perry Preschool Project, for example, numerous school districts are incorporating full- or half-day programs for preschoolers.

A number of states have enacted laws to implement early childhood education programs for economically disadvantaged children. Mitchell, Seligson, and Marx (1989) have documented the development of such programs, noting that the number of school-based early childhood education programs has increased significantly since 1985, as has the amount of state funds designated for them.

In addition to school improvement and early childhood education initiatives, this past decade has witnessed the emergence of family support programs. These programs provide support and guidance to families with infants and young children, often beginning the provision of services during the prenatal period (Weiss & Halpern, 1991). Although many family support programs are provided by community-based organizations, an increasing number of them, such as the Parents as Teachers program in Missouri, are administered by school districts. The services provided by such programs include parent education, health and developmental screening, and referral to services the parents or children may need. Since these programs focus on the prevention of developmental problems that may later hinder the child's ability to succeed in school, they may be considered within the context of school reform initiatives.

These school programs for improvement, early childhood, and family support vary in terms of their base of operation and the age of the children they serve, as well as in their approach to the problem. However, they share a common goal of addressing the needs of low-income children and preventing later social problems and academic failure. Although the programs are based in the school, they often recognize the importance of working with parents, and they include a focus on parent involvement. As Weiss and Halpern (1991) noted, most programs today are based on the premise—also emphasized in the School of the Future—that "the devastating effect of poverty is that it not only threatens infants' [and children's] physical well-being from the moment of conception, but simultaneously undermines the capacity of their parents to protect, nurture, and guide them" (p. 3).

A number of these programs have been evaluated and found to be effective in their approach (Schorr & Schorr, 1988; Price, Cowen, & Lorion, 1988), but they are not widely implemented, and usually only one or two services are provided in a school where the problems of children and their families are numerous and the need for many different services is apparent.

Implementation of the School of the Future: Some Cautions

The School of the Future incorporates many aspects of these and other innovative programs. It may be perceived not so much as a program but rather as a plan for the delivery and coordination of a range of different services. The program intends to address the needs of children from birth through adolescence. This wide age range is greater than that of most other programs. Some limit the age range of the children they serve to the prenatal period through age 12, while others may focus only on birth to age 3, the early childhood years, or the school-age years. In addition to a wide age range, the School of the Future differs from other programs in its attempt to offer "a full range of proven innovations," that promote self-esteem and positive human development as well as to coordinate a number of different types of services for children and their families.

Since the kinds of services that would be needed would vary depending on the age of the children as well as their families' circumstances, the intent to offer a comprehensive range of services is of vital importance. However, it does raise a question. Can so many services be implemented in the school? Although the traditional mission of the school is expanding to provide not only academic instruction but also a number of other services which address the mental health needs of children and their families, most schools would have difficulty implementing many different types of services. It could well be, therefore, that the School of the Future should adopt a building block approach to implementation. This stepwise approach would recognize the ultimate need for a comprehensive range of services, while encouraging schools to implement one or two services at a time, thus building a sound foundation before attempting to provide additional services.

Granted that the School of the Future calls for the implementation of a comprehensive range of services and innovative programs, it is important to note that no one is insisting upon immediate implementation. This plan to phase in services over a two-year period is advantageous, since it enables each site to proceed at its own pace, implementing services according to the site's needs, resources, and capabilities. In preparing the program for the step beyond a demonstration stage, it would be important to provide schools with some criteria and directions that would guide them in choosing among the services to be implemented initially.

The School of the Future calls not only for the provision of services but also for the coordination of services that exist in the community that the children and their families may need. In the communities of the demonstration sites there may be ample services which schools can draw upon, enabling children and their families to benefit. However, not all communities are equally blessed with a wide range of human services or with those services which families in the community need. The demonstration sites may be evaluated as effective because services are available, but would such effectiveness translate to schools in communities with fewer service resources?

Another concern is the amount of money that is needed to implement a full range of programs. The School of the Future is an experimental program. As such, it has some of the support as well as the connections and input from a variety of professionals from the Hogg Foundation and other organizations. This support has resulted in enthusiastic endorsement of the program both within and outside of the schools involved. As Holtzman notes in chapter 1, "Initiation of the four projects has unleashed a wide array of resources and activities that local school personnel, human service providers, and social agencies were ready to offer . . . . Long-range planning with the involvement of many partners at each site meant stability and reassurance that careful planning would pay off dividends in the long run" (p. 15).

Can such support be counted on when the program, if successful in the demonstration sites, is replicated elsewhere? How would schools generate such support? How much would it cost a school to implement a School of the Future model? These are questions that have to be addressed if the rationale underlying the Hogg Foundation's effort is not only to develop an experimental model school but also to develop one that can be widely replicated.

Developing flagship sites, as is the case with the School of the Future, is an approach taken by many innovative programs. In these cases, efforts are made not only to create a model program but also to evaluate it. Frequently in cases of model programs that have been evaluated as effective, questions arise about their widespread implementation. Weiss and Halpern (1991) addressed this issue:

The growing body of research documenting inter-site differences and program-site interactions raises critical questions for those formulating [programs]. How much is local ownership of a program and the flexibility to tailor a model to local circumstances prerequisite for program effectiveness and longevity? Can or should one "scale up," that is, replicate a specific program broadly? Or is it more appropriate to develop a general set of guidelines for programs to follow in creating local variants or new program models? (p. 26)

The Importance of Evaluation

These and other questions regarding the implementation of the program should be considered in the course of the program's evaluation. An important aspect of the School of the Future is the effort to undertake an evaluation of the program at each of the four experimental sites. Evaluation, defined as the systematic collection and analysis of data pertaining to the program (Cronbach, 1982), is now regarded as a necessary component of every model program. It is essential not only so that we may ascertain if the program is effective and should be continued and expanded but also in order that we may make necessary adjustments to the program as it evolves and use the results of the evaluation to obtain funds for the continuation or expansion of the program.

It is not possible to review the history of evaluation research within the limited scope of this chapter. Suffice it to mention that many changes have occurred and many lessons learned since the days of the Westinghouse evaluation of the Head Start program in 1969 (Travers & Light, 1982). Whereas two decades ago evaluators would have been satisfied with simply asking, Is the program effective? today they are more likely to ask, What aspects of the program are effective, to whom, and in what ways? (Zigler & Weiss, 1985).

Program evaluation now typically includes, as is the case with the School of the Future, both process evaluation (which seeks to examine what has been implemented, under what conditions, and how) and outcome evaluation (which focuses on the impact of the program). Of significance in the School of the Future is not only the inclusion of both types of evaluation but also the utilization of one type to inform the other. This point is made by Ellmer and Lein who note in chapter 2 that "descriptive information about differences in demographic, bureaucratic, program conception, or staffing patterns among sites could help explain programmatic and outcome measure differences that are expected to emerge" (p. 19).

Ellmer and Lein developed a schema for the design of the process evaluation, dividing the evaluation of the project into four phases: developmental, adoption, implementation, and institutionalization phases. However, it needs to be made clear at what point the project as a whole or the project in a particular site will change, for example, from an implementation phase to the institutionalization stage. It is also unclear if the phases refer to the process evaluation per se or to the project as it is implemented and evolves at each of the sites.

Many other programs use both process and outcome evaluation to monitor implementation and to document the programs' effects on the target populations. Some programs, one of these being the School of the 21st Century discussed later in this chapter, follow a five-tiered approach to evaluation developed by Jacobs (1988). The first level is a preimplementation phase where an attempt is made to collect data on the site and the community even before the program is initiated. Data from the site's needs assessment, often a prerequisite to an acceptance of a proposal for funding a site, may be used here. Level five is an outcome evaluation. The three levels in between––accountability level, program clarification level, and progress toward meeting objectives level—enable evaluators and program planners to ascertain which developmental stage the program has reached and the progress it has made toward meeting its goals and objectives.

This latter aspect is important since one of the lessons learned from two decades of program evaluation is the mistake of conducting an outcome evaluation prematurely. As Holtzman indicated in chapter 1, it takes considerable time to implement a program, especially one that is as comprehensive as the School of the Future, which includes not one but several different treatments and involves such a wide age range for the target population. Campbell (1987), who warned against conducting an outcome evaluation in the early stages of a program's development, suggested that we should not evaluate a program until "it is proud" (p. 347). Although an outcome evaluation should not be conducted too soon in the program's development, it is important to design an evaluation at the outset and, as is the case with the School of the Future, begin to collect baseline data before the program is implemented.

Another principle to keep in mind is that an evaluation should always be based on the goals of the project (Campbell, 1987). This point is emphasized since at times there is a discrepancy between the intent of a program or policy and its actual implementation (Lasswell, 1971). This fact points out the need to document, in a process evaluation, what services are actually being delivered, to whom, and in what ways. The goals of the School of the Future project have been enunciated at the outset and are no doubt included in various documents describing the program. However, site coordinators, principals, school board members, and other participants may have a different understanding of the goals and objectives of the project and may, indeed, work toward somewhat different ends. As part of the process evaluation it may be useful for interviewers to ask participants what they think the goals and objectives of the project are, and to do so at each stage of the process evaluation. To the extent that there is a discrepancy between the original intent of the program and how it is perceived by participants, a reorientation for some staff members (or changes in the evaluation design) may be necessary.

Another function of the process evaluation is to document the community context and the relationship between each of the schools and other service providers in the community. As noted earlier, communities differ in the availability of health, mental health, and social services for children and families. A careful documentation of what exists in the community at different phases of the evaluation may help in understanding not only the influence of the local context on the effectiveness of the program in a particular site (Weiss & Halpern, 1991) but also the influence of the project on the community. For example, activities associated with the School of the Future may alert local or state officials to the needs of low-income children, resulting in funds for additional services in that community. If this occurs, it should be considered a positive outcome of the School of the Future initiative.

In terms of the outcome evaluation plans as detailed in chapter 3, several strengths are immediately apparent. One is the selection, at the outset, of 10 control schools which will enable the evaluators to make some comparisons. In making such comparisons, however, it may be useful to look not only at student measures in the control schools but also at the local context and the services available to the control group. The control schools may not have a School of the Future project, but the students in those schools may receive similar treatment(s) elsewhere in the community. Lack of knowledge of services available to the control group could lead to misinterpretation of the findings.

Also important is the project's recognition of the length of time it takes programs to stabilize and the focus on both short-term and long-term outcomes for the project. Another strength of the evaluation is the inclusion not only of mental health and achievement measures but also measures of physical health. The interplay between these three areas is well documented, but one or another of these is often overlooked in an evaluation, depending on the focus of a particular program.

Several strengths are associated with the outcome evaluation of the School of the Future, but there is at least one serious flaw that should be corrected: a focus on students but no indication that data will be collected on the family. The School of the Future focuses not only on the needs of children but also on the needs of the family as a whole. However, from the description of the outcome evaluation to date, there seems to be not as much effort devoted to examining the program's impact on the family. For example, data will be collected on parent involvement, but this appears to be limited to process information—such as, Do parents attend evening classes? Are parents involved in school activities?—as opposed to the effect of parent involvement on the parents themselves as well as on the children. Like many other programs, the School of the Future has taken an ecological approach where the emphasis is not only on the child but on the child's development within a context of the family and the community (Bronfenbrenner, 1977; Zigler & Weiss, 1985). This ecological approach needs to be evident in the evaluation as well, which would need to include an examination of the effects of the program on parents.

The use of broader measures that go beyond measuring cognitive and other changes in the child is recognized by many researchers today. For example, in a longitudinal evaluation of one intervention, Seitz, Rosenbaum, and Apfel (1985) have assessed not only the program's impact on the child's development and educational progress but also the impact of the program on parents' welfare dependence and education.

Learning From Other Programs

Program planners have an opportunity not only to learn about other program evaluations but also to learn from and to contribute to the implementation of other school-based programs. As noted previously, many innovative programs have been developed in recent years, and some of these have contributed to the conceptual underpinnings of the School of the Future.

The School of the 21st Century. One such program is the School of the 21st Century (Zigler, 1987) which is a school-based child care and family support program with two major child care components: (1) all-day child care for children ages three, four, and five years and (2) before and after school and vacation care for children in kindergarten through sixth grade.

These child care services are provided five days a week (in one of the sites in Colorado, the program is open seven days a week), year round. Hence the School of the 21st Century not only extends the school year, it also extends the school day, requiring the use of the school building from as early as 6 a.m. to as late as 6 p.m.

In addition to the two child care components, the School of the 21st Century includes three outreach components: (1) home visitation and guidance to parents with children zero–three years of age (modeled after the Parents as Teachers program), (2) an information and referral component to assist parents in finding services they may need, and (3) outreach to and support of family day care providers in the neighborhood of the school. This latter component is included in view of the fact that family day care is the most prevalent form of out-of-home child care, especially for infants (U.S. Department of Labor, 1988). However, it is also the least supported and monitored form of out-of-home care (Kamerman & Kahn, 1987). Although some family day care providers participate in training activities offered in the community, many of them lack training, and they operate underground (Finn-Stevenson & Ward, 1990; Shuster, Finn-Stevenson, & Ward, 1991).

The School of the 21st Century programs identify family day care homes in the neighborhood of the school and invite providers to participate in training workshops and other activities. In this component, the school may be seen as the hub that enables providers to get to know and learn from one another and from other professionals. Since the child care providers are determinants of the kind of care the children receive, enabling them to participate in training is likely to have a positive effect on the experiences of children under their care (Phillips, 1989).

The School of the Future and the School of the 21st Century share some common elements. For example, both programs focus on the use of the school for the delivery of a wide range of services to children and their families and the provision of services beginning at the birth of the child, or even earlier. Also, both programs share an overarching goal—to enhance the lives and ensure the optimal development of children (Holtzman, this volume; Zigler, 1987; Zigler & Finn-Stevenson, 1989).

The School of the 21st Century was conceptualized as a response to the child care crisis our nation is experiencing (Zigler & Lang, 1991) and the stress and need for social support among young families. Unlike the School of the Future, which targets low-income children, the School of the 21st Century was conceptualized as a program that would address the needs of both poor and nonpoor families. Lack of child care, divorce, single-parent household, and teen pregnancy and parenthood are examples of some of the conditions affecting families. Although these conditions occur with greater frequency among low-income families (National Center for Children in Poverty, 1990), they also affect other children as well. This universality of need is especially the case with regard to child care services. The National Child Care Staffing Study (1990) found for example that a significant portion of children from middle-income families are in poor-quality child care centers, which may undermine the children's development.

In the School of the 21st Century the child care services are paid by parents on a fee-for-service basis, but special provisions—namely, a sliding scale fee system and subsidies—are built in to ensure that low-income children have access to the program. In conceptualizing the program, Zigler (1987) also underscored the importance of having an integrated program so as to avoid a two-tier system of child care which segregates children on the basis of their families' ability to pay for services. The School of the 21st Century, while conceptualized as a universal program that will become an integral part of the educational system, is not mandatory. It is utilized only by families needing the services.

To date, close to 200 schools in 8 states have implemented the School of the 21st Century program. Schools have the responsibility for making available or raising the start-up and operational funds needed. In some cases funds are provided by community foundations and corporations. In several states—Connecticut, Florida, and Kentucky are examples—state funds for the development of the program have been provided through enabling legislation. Although the program was conceptualized at the Yale Bush Center, the sites are not chosen by the center; rather, the schools express an interest in developing the program and the Bush Center, under the leadership of Zigler and Finn-Stevenson, provides them with technical assistance and training.

The Bush Center in the School of the 21st Century program plays an important role on at least five levels: (1) *conceptualization* of the idea, (2) *design* of the program, (3) the provision of *technical assistance and training* to facilitate the implementation of the program, (4) the *evaluation* of the program in several sites, and (5) ongoing *dissemination* of information about the program.

Finally, although the term "program" is used to describe the School of the 21st Century, like the School of the Future, the School of the 21st Century is not a program per se as much as it is a design for the delivery of a continuum of services to children and their families. As Zigler (1987) noted, there is nothing new about these services, some of which already exist in most, if not all, communities although only to a limited extent. However, the School of the 21st Century provides the blueprint for the development of an umbrella that brings these services together under the aegis of the school. It also includes a set of principles, drawn on the basis of what we know from developmental research and the evaluations of such programs as Head Start, which guide the implementation of child care and family support services in the schools.

Rather than develop a model School of the 21st Century site where implementation and evaluation of the program may take place under reasonably controlled circumstances, the School of the 21st Century utilizes a service-oriented approach which seeks widespread implementation at the outset. In helping schools implement the programs, no effort is made to provide them with a prototype for a model School of the 21st Century program. Rather, schools are given suggested services to be implemented and a set of guidelines and principles which give direction for the implementation of the services.

In part, the decision to opt for a service-oriented approach as opposed to the development of a model program in one or several flagship demonstration sites was driven by the sheer need for child care services and the interest of parents as well as educators to respond locally to the child care crisis. Having taken this approach, the task of the Bush Center in terms of program development was twofold. The first task was to develop guidelines for the implementation of the program as well as to ascertain, on the basis of review and analyses of other school-based programs, potential obstacles that implementors may face and ways they can circumvent them. For example, in any school, there exists the possibility that some teachers and other school personnel will resent new programs, consider nonteaching staff as intruders, and view the money devoted to new programs as displacing resources they need to teach children. Although schools also have many supporters of new programs among the teaching staff, even just a few opponents can detract from the success of the effort. This problem has been encountered not only by planners of school-based child care programs but also by planners of school-based health clinics. It can sometimes be prevented, or at least lessened, if efforts are made at the outset to involve teachers in the initial plans.

A second task was to develop the infrastructure necessary to enable schools to implement the program. For example, a School of the 21st Century Division was created within the Yale Bush Center to undertake the responsibility of providing information, orientation workshops, and technical assistance and training at several different levels. Also, a number of implementation and training manuals were developed and disseminated, thus enabling school officials to understand the concept underlying the program and the requirements associated with its implementation.

There are advantages to the service-oriented approach to program development, implementation, and evaluation. It enables each site to develop a variation of the program that is based on a needs assessment, is tailored to the idiosyncracies and circumstances as found in the particular site, and uses the resources available in the community. In evaluating the program, a basic evaluation design is used, incorporating both process and outcome evaluation, but the evaluation design is tailored to the specific site (Linkins & Finn-Stevenson, 1991).

There are limitations as well as advantages to this service-oriented approach to implementation and evaluation. For example, there is no one "model" School of the 21st Century program although there are several variants of the program in a number of different suburban, rural, and urban areas. Since the programs differ not only in terms of the community context but also in other respects as well, such as their source of funds (for example, whether they are publicly funded or supported by private funds), it is not possible to draw comparisons across sites.

New Beginnings. Another program which may be examined within the context of discussions on the School of the Future is New Beginnings, a program implemented in San Diego, California. New Beginnings is an approach to integrated services for children and families developed by the City and County of San Diego, San Diego Community College District, and the San Diego Public Schools. These agencies realized that they served the same families, who are often unaware of the existence of services. There was also a realization that families must go to several different agencies to solve multiple problems or to receive help with many pieces of a particular problem.

A needs assessment and feasibility study (Hickey, Lockwood, Payzant, & Wenrich, 1990) was conducted by the above-noted agencies confirming the problems families and children face in locating and receiving services. It was also ascertained that families perceive the school as a place to get help. To this end, New Beginnings uses the school as a primary source of referrals. However, services are not delivered in the school but in the Center, a separate place where two levels of services are provided: (1) an expanded student registration/family assessment process for all families and (2) service planning, ongoing case management and various health services for targeted families who need intervention. At the Center, families are also able to receive direct services which may include, for example, developmental screening, immunizations, and treatment for common childhood conditions as well as a range of family support services.

Although the school is only used as a referral source, classroom teachers receive intensive training in problem identification and supportive techniques and are informed of the services available at the Center. Ongoing communication between the teachers and Center staff is considered of vital importance in determining the beneficial effects of the services on the children and their families.

In the identification of the problem involving multiple service needs of families, New Beginnings is not unusual, being similar to the School of the Future. Like the School of the Future, New Beginnings also recognizes that access to services should begin at the school. However, a unique aspect of New Beginnings is its approach to ensuring that agencies work together in a cost-efficient manner. It was established at the outset that fragmentation of funding contributes to fragmentation of services. New Beginnings therefore uses existing agencies' resources as a primary source of funding, but reallocates the money in a more flexible and fiscally efficient manner. It is expected that the reduction in duplication of services by different agencies will result in cost savings.

The pooling of different agencies' resources is evident in the Center which is staffed by Family Services Advocates (FSAs). This represents essentially a redefinition of roles within the different agencies, since the FSAs remain on the staff of their "home agency" but work in the broader context and with other FSAs from other agencies at the Center. It is too early to tell if New Beginnings' approach to integrating services is successful. Since school personnel in the School of the Future will need to resolve the issue of how to provide and coordinate a wide range of different services, program planners should monitor the development of New Beginnings.

Conclusion

As we have seen in this chapter, the School of the Future is based on and is similar to several other school reform and family support initiatives. However, it targets a wider age range of children and their families and it seeks to provide a wider range of services in an integrated manner. Although the wide age range and comprehensive set of services render the project unique, they may also present problems in implementation and evaluation. Some of these problems have been identified herein. They are not insurmountable, and may be present only because the program is still in the developmental stage.

Two other programs in their initial stages of implementation—the School of the 21st Century and New Beginnings—were also discussed in this chapter in view of the fact that they share with the School of the Future a similar conceptual base. Likewise they involve the school either for the provision of services, as is the case with the School of the 21st Century, or as a source of referral, as is the case with New Beginnings. All three programs, although similar in their conceptual basis, have taken a different approach to implementation. A vital aspect of all three programs is that they include an evaluation of their effort. As such they are likely to contribute significantly to our store of knowledge regarding programs for low-income families and the use of the school to address the needs of children and their families.

References

Bronfenbrenner, U. (1977). Toward an experimental ecology of human development. American Psychologist, 32, 513-531.

Campbell, D. (1987). Problems for the experimenting society in the interface between evaluation and service providers. In S. L. Kagan, D. R. Powell, B. Weissbourd, and E. Zigler (Eds.), America's family support programs: Perspectives and prospects (pp. 345–351). New Haven, CT: Yale University Press.

Committee for Economic Development. (1987). Children in need: Investment strategies for the educationally disadvantaged. New York: Author.

Comer, J. (1991). African American children and the school. In M. Lewis (Ed), Child and adolescent psychiatry: A comprehensive textbook (pp. 1084–1091). Baltimore, MD: Williams & Wilkins.

Cronbach, L. J. (1982). Designing evaluations of educational and social programs. San Francisco, CA: Jossey-Bass.

Finn-Stevenson, M., & Ward, P. (1990). Outreach to family day care: A national volunteer initiative. Zero to Three, 10 (3), 18–21.

Hickey, N. W., Lockwood, J., Payzant, T. W., & Wenrich, J. W. (1990). New Beginnings: A feasibility study of integrated services for children and families. (Final report). San Diego, CA: County of San Diego, Office of the Chief Administrative Officer.

Jacobs, F. (1988). The five tier approach to evaluation: Context and implementation. In H. B. Weiss & F. Jacobs (Eds.), Evaluating family support programs (pp. 37–68). New York: Aldine De Gruyter.

Lasswell, H. D. (1971). A preview of policy sciences. New York: American Elsevier Publishing Co.

Linkins, K. & Finn-Stevenson, M. (1991). Report on the evaluation of the Connecticut Family Resource Centers. Unpublished. Submitted to the Connecticut Department of Human Resources, Hartford.

Mitchell, A., Seligson, M., & Marx, F. (1989). Early childhood programs in the public schools. Dover, MA: Auburn House.

National Center for Children in Poverty. (1990). *Five million children: A statistical profile of our poorest young children.* New York: Columbia University, School of Public Health.

National Child Care Staffing Study (1990). *Who cares for your child care providers and the quality of care in America?* (Final report). Washington, DC: Child Care Employee Project.

Phillips, D. (Ed.). (1989). *Quality child care: What the research tells us.* Washington, DC: National Association for the Education of Young Children.

Price, R. H., Cowen, E. L., & Lorion, R. P. (Eds.). (1988). *Fourteen ounces of prevention: A casebook for practitioners.* Washington, DC: American Psychological Association Press.

Schorr, L. B., & Schorr, D. (1988). *Within our reach: Breaking the cycle of disadvantage.* New York: Doubleday.

Seitz, V., Rosenbaum, L., & Apfel., N. (1985). Effects of family support intervention: A 10-year follow-up. *Child Development,* 56, 376–391.

Shuster, C., Finn-Stevenson, M., & Ward, P. (Eds.). (1991). *Family day care: Facing the hard questions.* New York: National Council of Jewish Women.

Slavin, R. E., Madden, N. A., Karweit, N. L., Livermon, B. J., & Lawrence, D. (1990). Success for all: First-year outcomes of a comprehensive plan for reforming urban education. *American Educational Research Journal,* 27, 255–278.

Travers, J., & Light, R. (Eds). (1982). *Learning from experience: Evaluating early childhood demonstration programs.* Washington, DC: National Academy Press.

U.S. Department of Labor. (1988). *Child care: A workforce issue.* Washington, DC: Author.

Weiss, H. B., & Halpern, R. (1991). *Community based family support and education programs: Something old or something new?* (Working paper). National Center for Children in Poverty. New York: Columbia University, School of Public Health.

Zigler, E. F. (1987, September). *A solution to the nation's child care crisis: The School of the 21st Century.* Paper presented at the opening of the 10th Annual Policy Luncheons in Child Development and Social Policy. New Haven: Yale University, Bush Center in Child Development and Social Policy.

Zigler, E. F., & Finn-Stevenson, M. (1989). Child care in America: From problem to solution. *Educational Policy,* 3, 313–329.

Zigler, E. F., & Lang, M. (1991). *Child care choices.* New York: MacMillan.

Zigler, E. F., & Weiss, H. B. (1985). Family support systems: An ecological approach to child development. In N. Rappoport (Ed.), *Children, youth and families: The action research relationship* (pp. 166-205). New York: Cambridge University Press.

CHAPTER 5

School-Based Service Integration:
Program Design and Evaluation Considerations

by

Margaret C. Wang

Contemporary school-community collaboration programs like the School of the Future project often are designed to provide a coordinated, shared responsibility approach to education and related health and human service delivery. A central concern of such programs is how educators and people in various organizations can enhance one another's efforts to improve the prospects and life circumstances of children, youth, and families in inner-city communities. Most such projects are, however, in their infancy. In every aspect of these emerging programs, help is needed in summarizing existing knowledge and in framing approaches to solving coordination and other implementation-related problems. An area that requires major attention at this early stage is a conceptual framework for organizing the wide array of variables considered by local projects in developing their site-specific programs. Beyond that, the framework can contribute significantly to building a systematic knowledge base on the design, planning, and implementation processes associated with school/community projects.

Discussion in this chapter focuses on the program design and evaluation plan of the School of the Future project in the context of contemporary education and social service reform efforts. Included also is a discussion of a conceptual model of variables that are important to learning that serves as a basis for guiding design and evaluation of school/community collaboration programs.

Program Design Considerations

Providing coordinated school-based health and social services that are targeted to serve children and families as a way to improving learning outcomes of children in a variety of at-risk circumstances has become a major focus of education and social service reforms of the 1990s. Although we have made great progress in ensuring free public education for all children, we have made far less progress in attaining equity in educational outcomes. Many students experience serious difficulties in achieving learning success, and they need better help than they are now receiving (Heller, Holtzman, & Messick, 1982; Kirst, 1991; Wang, Reynolds, & Walberg, 1988). Providing opportunities for students to receive an education without also ensuring desirable educational outcomes is one of the reasons the public is demanding more educational accountability.

School of the Future projects are among the most recent efforts in this nation's long-standing commitment to the goal of building an educated citizenry and as a means of achieving social and economic equity. The goal of equity in education can be traced back at least as far as 1776 and the beginning of the American Revolution. As Tyler (1985) noted:

> The American nation was founded by people who visualized a society in which everyone would be both a ruler and a worker. They believed that through education, all of the citizens of the new nation would learn what was necessary to be intelligent rulers.... [L]eaders of the American Revolution knew the wide range of individual differences in human populations . . . . Nevertheless, they believed that the desire for a democratic community and the dedication of effort to build such a nation would ensure that each citizen acquired the necessary knowledge, skills and attitudes. (pp. ix–x)

While this vision has remained a guiding principle for education in this country, its realization has been elusive. Schools today are challenged to serve an increasingly diverse student population. Research suggests that there is a wide range of ways in which students acquire, organize, retain, and generate knowledge and skills; it also indicates that economic, political, and demographic change have a significant impact on the ways in which education and related health and human services are provided. These differences and changes are not static, and, as noted by Holtzman in chapter 1, they are closely tied to each child's development as well as to the complex ecosystems in which children and their families live.

Barriers to Progress

Many young people today are connected only tenuously to their parents and lack healthy contacts with other adults. The schools and human service agencies designed to serve them are fragmented and uncoordinated. Despite the need for greater collaboration among the schools and relevant segments of the community, broad-based research to address the problems of fragmentation and inadequacies in the current service delivery systems is rare (Kirst & McLaughlin, 1990; Wang, et al., 1988). Professionals from different fields and disciplines tend to go their own way, read only their own literature, and theorize from their own perspectives. While such professionals presumably have both reason and opportunities for collaboration across disciplines, there have been few collaborative efforts in research and development to improve the life circumstances of inner-city children and youth.

Local schools and related social service agencies are faced with two demanding tasks: first, obtaining information on the design, implementation requirements, and efficacy of innovative practices and model programs, and second, determining criteria for evaluating the feasibility and appropriateness of programs to best serve the needs of a particular school or school district. There is a pressing need for detailed information on program design and implementation, but there is very little systematically organized information on demonstrably effective practices. Without such data it is difficult for parents, schools, and the community at large to make informed choices in selecting programs to meet their particular goals and needs.

A Shared Responsibility Approach to Service Delivery. The schools will continue to have primary responsibility for the formal education of our children and youth. However, exciting new modes of cooperation and collaboration between schools and organizations outside the school systems are being explored across the country to enhance the educational outcomes of the nation's children. An underlying premise of these new efforts, the School of the Future among them, is the belief that improving the capacity for education is a shared responsibility among families, schools, and the community.

The design, implementation, and evaluation of the School of the Future project at the four pilot sites in Texas will generate a much-needed knowledge base on how to use systematically what works in school-based service integration projects. Two features of the School of the Future project are particularly noteworthy: first, a set of design guidelines drawn from well-established programs such as Comer's (1985) School Development Program and Zigler's (1989) School of the 21st Century that emphasize community renewal, family preservation, and child development; and second, a planning process that mandates active involvement of all stakeholders in the identification and development of site-specific approaches at each of the four participating sites. Preliminary findings on the initial implementations in the pilot schools suggest a pattern of unique programming directions based on site-specific strengths, needs, and constraints. Perhaps more importantly, implementation at the four sites also reflects a shared goal of mobilizing and pooling community expertise and resources to meet effectively the needs of children, youth, and families.

While it is too early to draw any conclusion from the work of the School of the Future project, the design and initial implementation of the project suggest several emerging patterns that are also salient in the research literature on the design requirements of school/community connection projects (Scannapieco & Wang, 1991). They include, for example, design guidelines such as:

1. Services needed by children, youth, and their families should be provided in a continuing fashion, without artificial discontinuities. This suggests an important vertical coordinating function, or coordination through time, as well as horizontal or cross-agency coordination.
2. Dedicated staff should be provided to initiate and maintain coordinated efforts across agencies. Such coordination requires commitment, time, and effort.
3. Educators must be prepared to conduct services or programs in a variety of settings, expanding beyond traditional arrangements. This may require major structural and attitudinal changes that will take time and education.
4. If services are to be used, good communication is essential between programs and the persons they are designed to serve. Basic information about programs must be spread in every community, and steps must be taken to inspire trust and confidence in the personnel and agencies involved.
5. All kinds of community resources and expertise, including those from universities and public and private sector agencies, should be sought in implementing multidisciplinary service integration projects.

New agencies have been created in some cities to promote the coordinated involvement of businesses, labor unions, health-related resources, social agencies, and schools. Often housed in the mayor's office or under the city council, these programs have the potential to reach those at greatest risk by mobilizing public and private sector resources to enhance the community's education system. Table 1 provides a sample list of the types of school/community connection programs that are being created or are in operation in many cities across the country (Wang, 1990). However, such programs are quite new and are still seeking feasible ways to build connecting mechanisms for effective communication and coordination in service delivery. In every aspect of these emerging activities, help is needed in summarizing existing knowledge and in framing approaches to problems that involve research and evaluation.

Table 1

An Illustration of Design Elements of Extant School-Community Connection Programs

Program Types	Design Elements
Parent and child care education	Working with personnel from health and social service agencies to define the curriculum schools offer, both in- school classes and post-school programs sponsored by a variety of public and private sector agencies.
Health care and clinics	In cooperation with other agencies, schools conduct health training and participate in programs relating to children and youth at pre-compulsory and post-compulsory levels. Schools cooperate with other agencies in operating and using health clinics which deal broadly with health concerns of youth, including drug abuse prevention and the use of contraceptives to prevent unintended pregnancies.
Quality child care at precompulsory level	Schools lead in providing programs for children of teen parents who attend school. Schools participate in staffing and programming of child care units operated outside of schools. Child care programs are used as sites for training (practicums) and part-time employment by youth engaged in school-based training programs in child care.
Precompulsory early education	Schools lead in organizing early education programs for all children, including those with special needs. Programs are often located in or near sites of parents' employment and involve close collaboration of schools with other agencies, both public and private. In cooperation with other agencies, educators make special efforts to work toward preventing child abuse and neglect in high-risk situations.

Education for teenage parents	In cooperation with other agencies, school personnel design and lead programs for educating teenage parents, including both mothers and fathers.
School readiness	In cooperation with representatives of social agencies, churches, and other institutions, schools help parents and families to support school readiness activities (phonological awareness, storytelling, reading, community experience, language development, cooperative play, etc.)
Elementary education	Schools lead in strong programs in areas of cultural imperatives—especially in reading, arithmetic, and social skills. Strong efforts are made to involve families, churches, and other agencies to provide massive, high-quality experiences in the "imperatives" to all children. Special efforts are made in schools to coordinate across all categorical or special programs and the general offerings in the regular classrooms.
Middle school	In cooperation with community agencies of all kinds, schools offer experiences to students in "cultural electives." For example, students may visit and learn in TV stations, newspaper plants, hospitals, stores, industrial plants, government offices, transportation centers, etc. Efforts are made by school leaders to create contacts for students according to demonstrated interests and abilities. Hopefully, community representatives (from various businesses and other agencies) will establish continuing relationships for mentoring, motivating, employing (part-time), and supporting individual students—in cooperation with families and schools.
Secondary school	In cooperation with other agencies, schools will facilitate continuing mentorships by people of the community, part-time employment of students in ways that enhance career planning and education, and orientation to various vocations and professions that involve extensive preparation. Secondary schools will create attractive, practical programs in conjunction with vocational schools, community colleges, and other higher-education institutions to facilitate efficient transitions of students into the post-compulsory years. Schools plan and conduct specifically targeted training programs to encourage employment of youth from poor and/or ethnic and/or language minority backgrounds by otherwise reluctant employers.
Family-life education	Schools participate with churches, social agencies, and others in training parents on family life. Specifically included would be elements to encourage and prepare parents to be active partici-

pants in schools and elsewhere in advocating for their children.

Continuing education — The schools participate with other agencies, including businesses, vocational schools, and others, in operating life-long education for adults, particularly those who dropped out of school or graduated from secondary schools unprepared for gainful employment. This may well include curricular components relating to cultural enrichment and enjoyment as well as those relating specifically to competency for employment and community life.

Special services — Schools participate in planning and conducting special programs for people of the inner city who experience extraordinary difficulties, such as education in detention centers and prisons, mental health services for disturbed and mentally ill persons, and consultation for parents of disabled children. This specifically includes support of self-help groups such as groups of parents of disabled pupils or groups of formerly mentally ill persons, etc.

Program Evaluation Considerations

Innovative programs are designed and implemented to achieve specified outcomes. It is vital, especially during implementation of a new program, to provide adequate resources to determine whether and to what degree project objectives are achieved. Systematic documentation and evaluation are central to the validation and refinement of innovative education programs. Beyond that, they can contribute significantly to data on the design, planning, and implementation processes associated with such projects.

Although there is a substantial research base on what makes learning more productive (cf. Kagan, Rivera, & Parker, 1991; Nettles, 1990; Wang, Haertel, & Walberg, 1990; Williams, Richmond, & Mason, 1986; Wittrock, 1986), little is available about the relative importance of distinct and interactive influences on improving the education and life circumstances of children and families. It is generally recognized that use of the traditional "treatment/yield" paradigm within classical experimental designs is a necessary, but not sufficient, condition to understand how and why innovative programs work. The classical pretest and posttest control group experimental designs, while useful from a conclusion-oriented evaluation research perspective, are not sufficient to address such process evaluation questions as: What elements of the program need to be implemented (and at what levels) to make the program work? What are the critical features of the program that should be observed to validate program implementation?

The process evaluation component discussed by Ellmer and Lein in chapter 2 provides a complementary data base on outcome evaluation. It addresses the concern of what is actually implemented and changing in the school in relation to the community including (a) the implementation processes that established the program; (b) the role of the principals and other school staff in ensuring program implementation; (c) the ways in which staff are involved in the planning, implementation, and evaluation of the school program; and (d) the effects of changes in school/leadership variables, such as the role of the principal, the social climate, and the allocation and scheduling of human and financial resources.

Data bases derived from process evaluations can be expected to provide information on the technical aspects of initiating and maintaining innovative programs as well as on methods for improving implementation research and evaluation. Such information is essential if programs are to be implemented widely. Potential program adopters and users must be able to determine not only expected program performance but also the nature of specific links between the implementation of each aspect of the program and its intended outcomes. Information is needed to further the understanding of what constitutes effectiveness and the conditions that influence it.

Some Methodological Concerns. Research on school and community connections in general and school-based service integration projects in particular suffer from several methodological concerns. First, there is a great deal more fragmentation than communality in the assumptions, definitions, questions, theories, procedures, and analytic tools which deal with school/community problems. Second, there has been insufficient opportunity for persons studying common problems in school/community connections to share understandings and discuss research questions and methodological considerations. Third, narrowly framed research questions by researchers from different disciplines and service delivery perspectives lead to findings that offer limited insight into complex, multifaceted problems involving service integration. Finally, but not least, is the need for a conceptual framework that underscores the importance of political contexts and community history and that points to the interdependent and transactional influences on the life circumstances of children, families, and communities.

Program evaluation can be viewed as a mechanism for systematically guiding the process of program improvement to increase desirable effects, reduce undesirable ones, and meet the changing needs of students, teachers, and other stakeholders. The basic goals and major components of efforts such as the School of the Future are likely to remain the same over many years. However, ways of achieving these goals and implementing the program components may change markedly. It is conceivable that after conducting program evaluations that include the goal of a data-based approach to program refinement and validation, the School of the Future programs in Austin, Dallas, Houston, and San Antonio may look quite different from their original design or current implementation. This evolutionary change is appropriate and desirable. Thus, program evaluation is an evolving process in a continuing cycle of systematic tasks integral to achieving specific program goals. In the case of the Schools of the Future project, program evaluation, particularly from a decision-oriented perspective, aims to contribute to expanding the knowledge base on how to initiate, refine, and maintain a school/community shared responsibility approach to schooling success.

A Conceptual Model of Variables That Are Important to Learning

To implement and evaluate neophyte school/community connection programs such as the School of the Future project, a conceptual framework is needed. This would not only facilitate program development and systematic descriptions of program implementation across sites but also serve as a way of identifying programming gaps, determining programming priorities, and identifying features, processes, and other conditions that influence effectiveness.

Several important models of learning were developed in the 1960s and 1970s, including those of Carroll (1963), Bruner (1966), Bloom (1976), Harnischfeger and Wiley (1976), Glaser (1976), and Bennett (1978). All of these models recognize the primary importance of student ability and include constructs such as aptitude, prior knowledge, and other characteristics of individual students such as perseverance, self-concept, and attitude toward school. This acknowledgment of important individual differences among learners stood in contrast to more narrow psychological studies of influences on learning, which generally treated individual differences as a source of error and focused on instructional treatment variables (Hilgard, 1964). Although the more recent models refined the ways in which student characteristics and instructional variables were defined and related to one another, their primary contributions have been in extending the range of variables considered. Findings from a research study of psychological models of educational performance by Haertel, Walberg, and Weinstein (1983) suggested, for example, that previous models of school learning neglected extramural and social-psychological influences.

The understanding of school learning was further advanced with the introduction of models that are responsive to student diversity and that emphasize accountability for schooling success of every student (Wang, Haertel, & Walberg, 1990). These models pay particular attention to variables related to service delivery systems and program implementation requirements. One example is the Conceptual Model of Variables That Are Important to Learning (Wang, 1990). This model has provided the conceptual basis for a program of research on school/community connections at the National Center on Education in the Inner Cities, an interdisciplinary research and development center at Temple University supported by the U.S. Department of Education's Office of Educational Research and Improvement.

The Conceptual Model of Variables That Are Important to Learning, as shown in Figure 1, is an interactive, multidimensional framework. School effectiveness is viewed as having both macro- and microlevel dimensions. The macrolevel factors encompass a variety of extra-school variables; the microlevel factors emphasize the school environment and effectiveness of instructional practices that include some consistent or replicable patterns of teacher behaviors and student achievement. When this broadly defined conceptual framework is used as a basis for program development and evaluation, "effectiveness" is defined in a variety of ways by school personnel and other stakeholders: policymakers responsible for the accountability of educational outcomes, parents and community members who have the financial and moral obligation to support the schools, and advocacy groups committed to promoting school improvements.

The notion that there are multidimensional and variable interactive effects that influence learning is supported by findings in the contemporary literature on cognitive-social-psychological research on learning, effective teaching, school effectiveness, and school change. The validity of using the person-environment-process-product paradigm is supported by research concerned with social psychological processes and attitudes (Bossert, 1979; Gordon, 1983; McCombs, 1981; Walberg, 1991; Zimmerman, 1986). In addition, patterns of interaction among program features, student and teacher behaviors, and student outcomes have been noted in studies of the differential effects among instructional approaches (Berliner, 1983; Brophy, 1986; Reynolds, 1989; Wang, Haertel, & Walberg, 1990). Brown, Bransford, Ferrara, and Campione (1983) pointed to the "readiness" of the field to move from learning models that address learner knowledge (i.e., the learning process and learning tasks in relative isolation) toward a model that addresses the more complex interactive processes of learning. A major assumption underlying the design of the Conceptual Model of Variables, as shown in Figure 1, is that failure to recognize the interactive influence of many variables on learning can hamper both research and practice aimed at improving student outcomes. The rationale for each of the different kinds of variables included in the model is briefly discussed below.

Extra-School Variables. Examples of extra-school variables listed in Figure 1 include community characteristics; district-specific policies, programs, and characteristics; characteristics of social service delivery systems; statewide policies and funding regulations; and federal regulations and special categorical programs. These categories are concerned with macro-level variables that often have a major influence on the design and implementation of a program (Lieberman & Miller, 1990; Mitchell & Cunningham, 1990). However, schools rarely play a direct role in making modifications to meet the implementation needs of the schools' programs.

Community variables often operate as contextual variables that are highly influential, site-specific constraints. Among these are size, locale, economic condition, ethnic composition, child and family service resources, and the presence of different types of business and civic organizations. Also influential are district-level policy (program priority, per student spending, promotion policy), policies and guidelines issued by state departments of education (statewide testing programs, funding policy, programmatic initiatives), and federal regulations (policies governing funding, programmatic monitoring systems). Research on learning suggests that distal policy variables are less important to schooling outcomes than quantity and quality of instruction, home environment, and student characteristics. Research on program implementation indicates that there are significant differences among schools in student learning and outcomes (Purkey & Smith, 1983; Wang, Haertel, & Walberg, 1990).

Student Characteristics. Although individual differences have long been accepted as important, the implications of learner characteristics for instruction and learning outcomes have changed over the past two decades. These changes center on the types of information on learner characteristics that are examined, the methods of assessment for evaluating student learning progress and outcomes, and the ways in which information on learner characteristics is interpreted and used in providing instruction. Among the significant developments has been an increased recognition of the alterability of certain personal and learning characteristics (Bloom, 1976). Prime

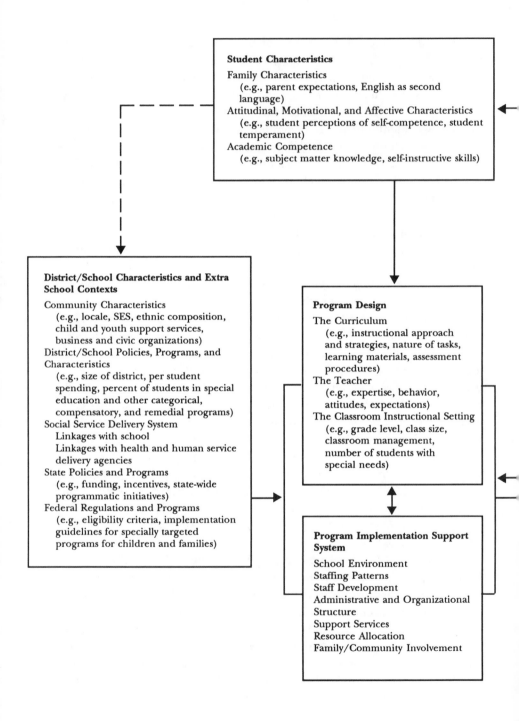

Degree of Program Implementation	Classroom Processes	Program Outcomes
Presence of Characteristics of the Classroom Learning Environment as Specified in the Program's Design	Teacher Behaviors (e.g., providing instruction, monitoring class work, evaluating student progress, providing feedback, behavioral management) Student Behaviors (e.g., patterns of the use of class time, task involvement, self-management, resource utilization, decision making relative to available options)	Student Learning Outcomes (e.g., task performance, basic subject-matter knowledge, ability to solve problems, positive attitudes about schooling and achievement motivation) Teacher Expertise and Attitude about Students and Their Learning Administrator/Instructional Leadership Expertise and Attitudinal Outcomes Family Attitude and Involvement Program Efficiency and Cost

Figure 1. Conceptual model of variables that are important to learning.

Note: Variables listed in this figure are intended to be illustrative only.

⟶ Program development and evaluation process

◀ — Feedback for program refinement and development

examples of variables that are no longer considered "static" include parental expectations and family involvement (Bronfenbrenner, 1986; Corno & Snow, 1986; Davis, 1991; Sternberg, 1990) and students' subject matter knowledge and learning skills (cf. Chipman, Segal, & Glaser, 1985; Wang, Reynolds, & Walberg, 1987; Wittrock, 1986).

Despite the research base that suggests a range of "alterable" individual-difference variables as correlates of learning, few of these variables are incorporated in the actual planning and delivery of instruction. (See sample list of learner characteristics considered in the research literature to be alterable and influential in the "Student Characteristics" box in Figure 1.) Current programs tend to be concerned with a limited number of learner characteristics, most of which relate to academic achievement as measured by standardized achievement tests. In only a few cases are such broad outcomes as ability to be self-directed, engage in cooperative learning, and seek and provide help explicitly featured in the curriculum or evaluated. One major reason for this gap is the lack of a descriptive data base on a broad range of instructionally relevant learner characteristics for instructional planning and assessment (cf. Freeman, 1988).

Program Design. Three categories of program design characteristics or variables—the curriculum, the teacher, and the classroom instructional setting—are listed in Figure 1. Since these variables are prominent in recent effectiveness research literature (Reynolds, 1989; U.S. Department of Education, 1986, 1987; Wang, Haertel, & Walberg, 1990; Waxman & Walberg, 1991; Wittrock, 1986), they should be considered in the design and study of programs to improve student outcomes.

The variable category "curriculum," as shown in Figure 1, is broadly defined to include specific learning tasks, curriculum, materials, and the approaches and activity structures within which instruction and learning take place. The "teacher" category, in the context of the model, refers to classroom teachers, as well as to specialized professionals such as special education teachers, speech therapists, school psychologists, and other related service providers and paraprofessionals who work directly with students in the instructional/learning process. Examples of teacher variables are expertise; attitudes toward students, the program, and the school; and expectations of self, self-perceptions of competence, and expectations of the effects of the program. The "classroom instructional setting" category includes such variables as physical design of the classroom, class size, student achievement levels, and the number of students identified as having special needs.

Improving the quality of education in schools is often an implicit goal in programs designed to increase school/community linkages or implement school-based services. However, broad-based approaches to school improvement tend to pay little attention to classroom instruction and subject matter learning. For example, it is clear that the ultimate goal of the School of the Future project is enhanced student learning outcomes. However, little reference has been made on the educational programs being implemented at project sites, nor are instructional/learning activities included as variables for the evaluation studies being planned. While it is expected that a program of the magnitude of the School of the Future project must direct its attention to selected priority areas, it must not overlook the best and most promising instructional practices while introducing other school-based support services.

The unsuccessful implementation of innovative school programs frequently has been attributed to a lack of well-defined implementation supports (Ellett & Wang, 1987; Fullan, 1985; Goodlad, 1984; Joyce, 1990; Kyle, 1985; Wang, 1984). Schools are complex organizational structures with well-established rules and norms of behavior. Successful efforts to improve student performance are nurtured by the school organization as a whole as well as by all of the interrelated components. One such component is support systems for program delivery or implementation (Figure 1) (Goodlad, 1987). The underlying assumption is that skillful program implementation requires effective use and management of all available resources. Granted that parent and community involvement is essential, the number of specialists and their time available to work with classroom teachers and students who require greater than usual instruction and related services and the amount of staff development and technical support also contribute in important ways to effective program implementation.

Program Implementation Support System. Successful program implementation requires changes in the total school environment to reinforce collaborative planning, cooperation, and teaming among the school staff, as well as leadership that supports instructional experimentation and accountability (Lieberman & Miller, 1990; Sergiovanni, 1990). Instructional teaming, for example, allows teachers to share their expertise. It enables them to use school time more effectively. Research suggests that students in classrooms with instructional teaming, compared to students in self-contained classrooms, tend to spend more of their school time receiving instruction (Goodlad, 1984; Stein & Wang, 1988; Williams et al., 1986). They also show improved self-concepts and attitudes toward school (Goodlad, 1984; Wang, Vaughan, & Dytman, 1985). In addition, teachers working in teams tend to provide a wider variety of coordinated instructional options.

Effectively educating students requires coordinated efforts by the instructional staff and professional service providers such as school psychologists, school social workers, and educational diagnosticians. Increased collaboration and consultation among these educators has become an important objective for achieving an effective, integrated system of service delivery especially in providing for the special learning needs of students who are mainstreamed in regular classes (Zins, Curtis, Graden, & Ponti, 1988).

Systematic staff development is another critical dimension. The effective operation of educational programs, especially new ones that provide a comprehensive and coordinated system of service delivery, requires ongoing staff development activities that promote understanding of the programs and that are directly related to day-to-day implementation. Findings from a number of development efforts have pointed to the importance of preservice and inservice staff development that adapts to the needs and talents of individual staff (Freiberg & Waxman, 1988; Fullan, 1985; Joyce, 1990; Showers, 1985; Vaughan, Wang, & Dytman, 1987).

Finally, the role of parents and other family members is a widely acknowledged, yet often neglected, support variable affecting program implementation. Students in even the best-designed and best-executed educational programs benefit greatly by encouragement at home. The active participation of parents and other family members in students' learning facilitates increased communication between school and home. Research shows that educational intervention programs designed to involve family members in significant ways are more effective than programs aimed exclusively at students (Bronfenbrenner, 1986; Davis, 1991; Mitchell & Cunningham, 1990).

Degree of Program Implementation. The extent to which a program is actually implemented is important in any evaluation for two reasons: (1) adequate descriptions of program effects require data on how well program design features are implemented as well as assessments of program outcomes and (2) a claim of successful implementation requires explicit information about a program's operating features and implementation conditions (Fullan, 1985; Wang, Nojan, Strom, & Walberg, 1984). A number of studies have suggested that exemplary educational interventions can have a substantial impact on schooling practice and student learning (Vaughan et al., 1987), but whether or not schools actually adopt such programs depends on a host of factors, including evidence of effectiveness and descriptions of conditions required for implementation. Both kinds of information are equally important.

A program with the most impressive evidence of effectiveness will not work unless staff actually implement it properly. When a new program is adopted, special care should be taken to ensure thorough understanding of the program's objectives and operating procedures. Firsthand reports of day-to-day operation and program impact help to answer questions such as: Do we have the personnel and other resources to operate the program? Would we like to see this program functioning in our school on a daily basis? Measures of the degrees of success with which specific program components have been properly implemented help to answer questions such as: Who does what to produce what mediating effects? In what contexts and under what conditions does program implementation best occur? What is the specific linkage between implementing each aspect of a program and its intended outcomes?

Classroom Processes. The mediating role of classroom processes in student learning is substantiated by findings from research designed to (a) examine the interactive effects of teacher and student behaviors in the classroom learning process, (b) detail the specific learning processes of individual students, and (c) describe the social context of learning. The inadequacy of certifying program effectiveness on the basis of student outcomes alone, without describing the processes and situations responsible for the outcomes, is well documented (Fullan, 1985). The primary categories of classroom process variables are student behaviors and teacher behaviors.

Student Learning Behaviors. In addition to the kinds of data that typically are collected in classroom process studies (e.g., teacher-student interactions), there are several specific student behaviors that are correlates of learning. These include task involvement, opportunities to respond, energy deployment, autonomy, time on task, and resource utilization and decision making. Recent developments in cognitive science point to the significant impact of metacognitive variables in student learning outcomes (McCombs, 1991; Reynolds, 1989; Wang, Haertel, & Walberg, 1990). Among these are comprehension monitoring (planning; monitoring effectiveness of attempted action; testing, revising, and evaluating learning strategies), self-regulatory and self-control strategies, and other highly rated student variables including positive behavior and ability to make friends among peers, participation in extracurricular school activities, motivation to achieve and aspirations for academic success, and perseverance in learning (Walberg, 1991).

Teacher Instructional Behaviors. An impressive amount of research during the past two decades has been devoted to teacher behavior, expertise, and effectiveness (cf. Wang, Reynolds, & Walberg, 1990; Wittrock, 1986).

Increasingly, particularly in research concerning teacher decision making and thinking, teachers are characterized as clinical diagnosticians who are expected to identify the learning needs of individual students and to make instructional decisions (preplanned or on-the-spot) that are adaptive to those needs. For example, among the variables in earlier studies that have been rated as important to learning are corrective feedback in case of student error, frequent academic questions, and accurate measurement of skills. The literature also indicates a strong relationship between student outcomes and the teaching of skills in the context of meaningful applications, use of good examples and analogies, and teaching for meaningful understanding, together with explicit promotion of student self-monitoring of comprehension and gradual transfer of responsibility for learning from the teacher to the student (Wang, Haertel, & Walberg, 1990).

Program Outcomes. Examples of program outcomes (Figure 1) are student academic, social, and attitudinal improvements presumed related to effective implementation of the program features. In addition to their function in contributing to other desired outcomes, these variables are valued program outcomes in and of themselves. As mentioned earlier, other important outcome variables for a program are improved expertise and attitudes of teachers and administrators and their expectations for such things as student improvement, orderly school climate, positive family attitudes about the school, involvement in monitoring student achievement, and participation in school activities.

Variables related to schooling processes respond to a multitude of influences, interacting in a variety of patterns, and lead to varied outcomes. Research suggests that a large number of the variables are moderately related to learning outcomes (Wang, Haertel, & Walberg, 1990), but few, if any, isolated variables prove to be strongly related to important student outcomes. Selected variables, however, when taken together, can be powerful determinants of school effects. Thus, a vital step in designing and planning program evaluation is defining the effects that the program is expected to produce. This step is necessary to avoid two pitfalls. The first is overlooking one or more important program outcomes. For example, program evaluations often use standardized achievement tests as the sole criterion of program effectiveness, despite the fact that innovative programs almost always have additional goals. The second pitfall is measuring outcomes that are unrelated or only tangentially related to program goals. Not only does this place an unwarranted strain on resources, but also important outcomes may be overlooked in a profusion of unnecessary data.

Conclusion

The School of the Future project has made considerable progress in a short time. As with most reform efforts with broad agendas, the project is faced with many, and often competing, demands. Strategic planning, responsible implementation, and above all, practical wisdom are required as the many dimensions of the project unfold.

Like the children and families being served by the School of the Future, innovative programs evolve in stages of development, growth, and change. Procedures found useful in one city can be helpful to others who are initiating similar programs elsewhere. Strong efforts are needed to encourage exploration, to share ideas on solutions to thorny problems, to identify promising practices, to analyze how programs are implemented, and to evaluate outcomes. The cross-city networking among the participants in the School of the Future is crucial to success. This kind of collaboration will contribute to sustained improvement in the participating communities and schools. The research and evaluation will yield a much-needed knowledge base on how to provide school-based services that are both feasible and effective in improving the education and life circumstances of children and their families living in high-risk environments.

References

Bennett, S. N. (1978). Recent research on teaching: A dream, a belief and a model. *British Journal of Educational Psychology, 48,* 127–147.

Berliner, D. C. (1983). Developing conceptions of classroom environments: Some light on the T in classroom studies of ATI. *Educational Psychologist, 18,* 1–13.

Bloom, B. S. (1976). *Human characteristics and school learning.* New York: McGraw-Hill.

Bossert, S. T. (1979). *Tasks and social relationships in classrooms.* New York: Cambridge University Press.

Bronfenbrenner, U. (1986). Ecology of the family as a context for human development: Research perspectives. *Developmental Psychology, 22,* 723–742.

Brophy, J. E. (1986). Research linking teacher behavior to student achievement: Potential implications for instruction of Chapter 1 students. In B. I. Williams, P. A. Richmond, & B. J. Mason (Eds.), *Designs for compensatory education: Conference proceedings and papers* (Vol. IV, pp. 121–179). Washington, DC: Research and Evaluation Associates.

Brown, A. L., Bransford, J. D., Ferrara, R., & Campione, J. (1983). Learning, remembering, and understanding. In J. H. Flavell & E. Markman (Eds.), *Mussen handbook of child psychology: Vol. 3. Cognitive development* (4th ed., pp. 77–166). New York: Wiley.

Bruner, J. S. (1966). *Toward a theory of instruction.* New York: Norton.

Carroll, J. B. (1963). A model for school learning. *Teachers College Record, 63,* 722–732.

Chipman, S. G., Segal, J. W., & Glaser, R. (Eds.). (1985). *Thinking and learning skills: Vol. 2. Research and open questions.* Hillsdale, NJ: Lawrence Erlbaum.

Comer, J. P. (1985, September). *The School Development Program: A nine step guide to school improvement* [Paper]. New Haven, CT: Yale Child Study Center.

Corno, L., & Snow, R. E. (1986). Adapting teaching to individual differences among learners. In M. C. Wittrock (Ed.), *Handbook of research on teaching* (3rd ed., pp. 605–629). New York: Macmillan.

Davis, D. (1991). School reaching out: Family, school, and community partnerships for student success. *Phi Delta Kappan, 72*(1), 376–382.

Ellett, C. D., & Wang, M. C. (1987). Assessing administrative and leadership components of program implementation in an innovative ECE program. *Journal of Research in Childhood Education, 2*(1), 30–47.

Freeman, E. F. (Ed.). (1988). *Assessment in the service of learning: Proceedings of the 1987 ETS Invitational Conference.* Princeton, NJ: Educational Testing Service.

Freiberg, H. J., & Waxman, H. C. (1988). Alternative feedback approaches for improving student teacher's classroom instruction. *Journal of Teacher Education, 33*(4), 8–14.

Fullan, M. (1985). Change processes and strategies at the local level. *Elementary School Journal, 85*(3), 391–422.

Glaser, R. (1976). Components of a psychology of instruction: Toward a science of design. *Review of Educational Research, 46,* 1–24.

Goodlad, J. I. (1984). *A place called school: Prospects for the future.* New York: McGraw-Hill.

Gordon, E. W. (Ed.). (1983). *Human diversity and pedagogy.* Westport, CT: Mediax.

Haertel, G., Walberg, H. J., & Weinstein, T. (1983). Psychological models of educational performance: A theoretical synthesis of constructs. *Review of Educational Research, 53*(1), 75–91.

Harnischfeger, A., & Wiley, D. E. (1976). The teaching-learning process in elementary schools: A synoptic view. *Curriculum Inquiry, 6,* 5–43.

Heller, K., Holtzman, W., & Messick, S. (Eds.). (1982). *Placing children in special education: A strategy for equity.* Washington, DC: National Academy of Sciences Press.

Hilgard, E. R. (1964). A perspective of the relationship between learning theory and educational practices. In E. R. Hilgard (Ed.), *Theories of learning and instruction: 63rd yearbook of the National Society for the Study of Education* (pp. 402–415). Chicago: University of Chicago Press.

Joyce, B. (Ed.). (1990). *Changing school culture through staff development: ASCD 1990 yearbook.* Alexandria, VA: Association for Supervision and Curriculum Development.

Kagan, S. L., Rivera, M., & Parker, F. L. (1991, January). *Collaborations in action: Reshaping services to young children and their families* [Executive summary]. New Haven, CT: Yale University, Bush Center in Child Development and Social Policy.

Kirst, M. W. (1991, April). Improving children's services: Overcoming barriers, creating new opportunities. *Phi Delta Kappan, 72*(8), 615–618.

Kirst, M. W., & McLaughlin, M. (1990). Rethinking policy for children: Implications for educational administration. In B. Mitchell & L. L. Cunningham (Eds.), *Educational leadership and changing contexts of families, communities, and school: 89th yearbook of the National Society for the Study of Education* (Part 2, pp. 69–90). Chicago: University of Chicago Press.

Kyle, R. M. (Ed). (1985). *Reaching for excellence.* Washington, DC: E. H. White.

Lieberman, A., & Miller, L. (1990). Restructuring schools: What matters and what works. *Phi Delta Kappan, 71*(10), 759–764.

McCombs, B. L. (1991). Motivation and lifelong learning. *Educational Psychologist, 26*(2), 117–127.

Mitchell, B., & Cunningham, L. L. (1990). *Educational leadership and changing contexts of families, communities, and schools.* Chicago: National Society for the Study of Education.

Nettles, S. (1990). *Community involvement; disadvantaged students: A review.* Baltimore: Johns

Hopkins University Center for Research on Effective Schools for Disadvantaged Students.

Purkey, S. C., & Smith, M. S. (1983). Effective schools: A review. *Elementary School Journal, 83*, 427–452.

Reynolds, M. C. (1989). *Knowledge base for the beginning teacher.* Oxford, England: Pergamon Press.

Scannapieco, M., & Wang, M. C. (1991). *Synthesis of the literature on inner-city school-community connection programs.* Philadelphia: Temple University Center for Research in Human Development and Education.

Sergiovanni, T. J. (Ed.). (1990). Adding value to leadership gets extraordinary results. *Educational Leadership, 47*(8), 23–27.

Showers, B. (1985). Teachers coaching teachers. *Educational Leadership, 42*(7), 43.

Stein, M. K., & Wang, M. C. (1988). Teacher development and school improvement: The process of teacher change. *Teaching and Teacher Education, 4*(2), 171–187.

Sternberg, R. J. (1990). Thinking styles: Key to understanding student performance. *Phi Delta Kappan, 71*, 366–371.

Tyler, R. W. (1985). Foreword. In M. C. Wang & H. J. Walberg (Eds.), *Adapting instruction to individual differences* (pp. ix–xii). Berkeley, CA: McCutchan.

U.S. Department of Education. (1986). *What works: Research about teaching and learning.* Washington, DC: Author.

U.S. Department of Education. (1987). *Schools that work.* Washington, DC: U.S. Government Printing Office.

Vaughan, E. D., Wang, M. C., & Dytman, J. A. (1987). Implementing an innovative program: Staff development and teacher classroom performance. *Journal of Teacher Education, 38*(6), 40–47.

Walberg, H. J. (1991). Enhancing school productivity: The research basis. In P. Reyes (Ed.), *Teachers and their workplace* (pp. 277–296). Newbury Park, CA: Corwin-Sage Publications.

Wang, M. C. (Ed.). (1984). Integration of students with special needs in regular classroom environments [Special issue]. *Journal of Remedial and Special Education, 14*(3).

Wang, M. C. (1990). *Center for Education in the Inner Cities* [Technical proposal]. Philadelphia: Temple University Center for Research in Human Development and Education.

Wang, M. C., Haertel, G. D., & Walberg, H. J. (1990). What influences learning? A content analysis of review literature. *Journal of Educational Research, 84*(1), 30–43.

Wang, M. C., Nojan, M., Strom, C. D., & Walberg, H. J. (1984). The utility of degree of implementation measures in program implementation and evaluation research. *Curriculum Inquiry, 14*(3), 249–286.

Wang, M. C., Reynolds, M. C., & Walberg, H. J. (Eds.). (1987, October). *Repairing the second system for students with special needs.* Paper presented at the Wingspread Conference, Racine, WI.

Wang, M. C., Reynolds, M. C., & Walberg, H. J. (1988). Integrating the children of the second system. *Phi Delta Kappan, 70*(3), 248–251.

Wang, M. C., Reynolds, M. C., & Walberg, H. J. (Eds.). (1990). *Special education: Research and practice: Synthesis of findings.* Oxford, England: Pergamon Press.

Wang, M. C., Vaughan, E. D., & Dytman, J. A. (1985). Staff development: A key ingredient of successful mainstreaming. *Teaching Exceptional Children, 17*(2), 112–121.

Waxman, H., & Walberg, H. (Eds.). (1991). *Contemporary research on teaching.* Berkeley, CA: McCutchan.

Williams, B. I., Richmond, P. A., & Mason, B. J. (1986). Designs for compensatory education: Conference proceedings and papers. Washington, DC: Research and Evaluation Associates.

Wittrock, M. C. (Ed.). (1986). *Handbook of research on teaching* (3rd ed.). A project of the American Educational Research Association. New York: Macmillan.

Zigler, E. F. (1989). Addressing the nation's child care crisis: The School of the 21st Century. *American Journal of Orthopsychiatry, 59,* 485–491.

Zimmerman, B. J. (Ed.). (1986). Discussion of role subprocesses in student self-regulated learning [Special issue]. *Contemporary Educational Psychology, 11*(4).

Zins, J. E., Curtis, M. J., Graden, J. L., & Ponti, C. R. (1988). *Helping students succeed in the regular classroom.* San Francisco: Jossey-Bass.

PART 2

CHAPTER 6

San Antonio Family Support Program:
Reflections on the School of the Future
in the Center of a Public Housing Project

by

Laura Lein, Patti Radle, & Rod Radle

In a neighborhood where home life often provides too few of the necessities for basic healthy survival—necessities such as food, clothing, shelter, security, stability, and affection—J.T. Brackenridge Elementary School, known in the community as J.T., serves as an oasis for many children. Children know the school will always be available to offer free breakfast and lunch, emergency clothes and shoes when possible, immediate medical attention, warm hallways and classrooms, and a safe haven from most negative influences and threats. For seven hours a day, children are housed in a building shared with caring adults, many of them teachers who have worked at J.T. for over a decade. Children's relatively high rates of attendance at the school indicate its attractiveness to them. J.T. ranks above average in attendance among the schools of the San Antonio Independent School District (SAISD), with a considerable improvement shown in the last four years according to the school's principal (Tobin, 1990). The San Antonio School of the Future project is located in this promising setting.

Background

The vast majority of the current 850 students enrolled at J.T. Brackenridge come from economically poor, Mexican-American families. According to 1989 statistics gathered by the Alazan/Apache Courts Housing Administration, the average annual income for a family of four in the school community is approximately $4,400. The population has a higher number of children and individuals over 65 years of age than most neighborhoods in the city. Research conducted by San Antonio Cares, a multiservice agency, indicates that the infant and neonatal death rates are up to four times those found in wealthier areas of the city. Fewer than 20 percent of the population have a high school education (San Antonio Cares, 1990).

The School of the Future project in San Antonio, Texas, is situated in the large modern J.T. Brackenridge Elementary School. The school, originally constructed in 1906, was entirely rebuilt in 1978. It has the capacity to serve 1,000 students. Two miles west of downtown San Antonio, the campus is within walking distance of both Tafolla Middle School and Lanier High School.

The school community is most closely associated and identified with the facility which houses the majority of its families. The Alazan/Apache Courts Housing Project, the oldest federal housing project in the nation, officially houses 1,000 families. Over 54 percent of the children in the community are residing in one-parent families. Unemployment is high. Family violence and substance abuse are frequent and overt. J.T. Brackenridge Elementary School is located adjacent to the housing project.

To many residents of San Antonio, the near west side, including the Alazan/Apache Courts, is an area to avoid. The area is known as a focus for prostitution, drugs, gang violence, and early death. This perception of danger in the community was reinforced graphically in June 1991. In a period of one week, four killings occurred in the Courts. Front page news reports reaffirmed to the wider San Antonio community that "random" killings and gang violence pervaded the neighborhood. With each successive killing the Alazan/Apache Courts were more visible to the city and the state as a setting for severe social problems, requiring quick solutions.

The city responded with a variety of Band-Aid measures to address the problem. The city council passed a youth curfew ordinance for the city. The housing authority opened discussions of lease clauses restricting guns and alcohol in the projects. The mayor called for churches to serve as collection points for illegal weapons. Rarely, especially in today's atmosphere of increasing taxes and decreasing services, were the roots of the problem addressed. Rarely were the killings seen as what they were—acts of family or drug-related violence. Rarely were the deaths described as the long-term consequences of multigenerational, persistent poverty.

Basis for the Project

J.T. Brackenridge Elementary has long held its position as a safe haven within the community. Parents and grandparents speak of past faculty and administrators in familiar terms. Many children are currently taught by teachers who taught their parents when they attended J.T. Graduates stop by after school in order to obtain attention from individuals whom they trust.

Although the school has a long history within the community, the School of the Future project utilized three assessment tools to identify directions parents and children proposed for the project. During the summer of 1988, Lein and her graduate students from the School of Social Work at The University of Texas at Austin completed intensive home surveys with 150 households from the Alazan/Apache Courts. The original research was designed to explore the impact of welfare and social service institutions, including the public schools, on the lives of children and their families. The following three findings emerged from her research (Lein, 1990):

1. *Formal counts of the community population in the census and in the public agency rolls do not accurately reflect the actual number and demography of community residents.* Many men are invisible to formal population counts. They live on the streets, or they are illegal residents of a housing unit legally occupied by a woman and children. Many men from poor families in the community are incarcerated. Not only men, but entire families may go uncounted. Often several families "share" the same unit. When families and individuals are not included in population counts, they likely are in no position to apply for and receive social services and benefits.

2. *Parents and children had trouble articulating goals and aspirations, as well as the pathways by which these might be achieved.* A large group of parents could articulate goals for their children only in negative form: "not dropping out," "not doing drugs," or "not going to jail." Other parents held high aspirations, hoping their children would become doctors, lawyers, or other highly paid professionals. However, parents had little understanding of the pathways by which children might achieve such goals. The lack of specific and realizable goals is both a consequence and a reinforcer of persistent poverty. Unless parents and children together can identify new goals, as well as the means to obtain them, children cannot progress along new pathways previously closed to them.

3. *Persistent poverty is maintained and strengthened by the complex local, state, and federal regulations controlling welfare programs.* Families spend inordinate amounts of time dealing with up to 20 or 25

service agencies. In so doing they spend much of their time waiting in line, "on hold" when telephoning, or traveling from one agency to another. Family members also learn that, in order to acquire the bare minimum needed for their family's survival, they will have to withhold the facts or lie, to break agency regulations, and to manipulate many agencies, each providing only a narrow range of services.

Based on these findings, an initial survey during the summer of 1990 by a social work intern of a sample of school families indicated their needs for different kinds of assistance. Families requested help in developing more effective parenting skills, assistance with social service agencies, and opportunities for more involvement in school activities. The range of topics raised in the 25 interviews indicated the need for a more extensive family survey to clarify the family needs and aspirations across the community.

Subsequent to this initial study, graduate students and social work interns worked together with a more formal survey instrument to gather demographic information on each household, as well as the parents' views of their neighborhood and school. The interview inquired more specifically concerning the need for services contributing to child and family mental health. Over a two-year period, project staff plan to complete an interview with each family having a child enrolled at J.T. Brackenridge. Social work and therapy interns from the project as well as graduate students under Lein's supervision have completed nearly 120 interviews to date, representing approximately 25 percent of the households with children enrolled.

Preliminary findings, taken from a sample of 20 of the completed interviews, reveal a desire by parents for more interaction with the school; a demand that teachers maintain higher expectations for their children; and a need for assistance in improving family life circumstances. More specifically, eight significant themes identified to date are the following:

1.   Parental desire for more information about what their children are actually learning; parents want especially to see more homework and graded papers;

2.   Parental requests for more parent/teacher conferences to allow them to keep abreast of their children's progress;

3.   More intensive and inclusive PTA activities;

4.   Parental requests for improvements to the school environment, including such activities as parent meetings, a community parade, more playground equipment, and more teacher respect

for the students;

5. Parental need for assistance in dealing with discipline problems such as getting children to school in the morning;

6. Parental need for assistance in weakening gang influence and dealing with drugs and teen pregnancy;

7. Parental need for GED classes, job training, and job placement; and

8. Parental need for help on a range of issues including the location of housing, dealing with family violence, and preventing substance abuse in the home.

Overall, parents wanted teachers to challenge their children in the classroom, and they, themselves, wanted to be more involved in their children's education. The parents expected teachers, and the school as an institution, to develop higher expectations for their children than they have held in the past. The needs described by parents have given the project a sense of immediate direction. All four programs implemented this year address parental concerns. Once the survey is complete, a thorough review of the findings will assure that parents' needs have been identified and are addressed in the most productive manner possible.

While research findings focused on parental needs and concerns, it is important to recognize that many adults expressed positive attitudes about the school, teachers, and education their children are receiving. Families continue to see the school as a "safe place," and family respect for the school contributes to the promise of benefits to be gained from future school-based programming.

Another survey, completed in the spring of 1991 with all fourth and fifth grade students, ascertained their knowledge of drugs and drug effects as well as their drug experience. Project staff compared results from J.T. Brackenridge with a districtwide survey completed the previous year. The results confirmed the experience of the staff in the School of the Future therapy program, one of the new services that has been implemented. With the exception of inhalant abuse, students reported drug experimentation or utilization at rates comparable to or lower than districtwide rates for students. On the other hand, students reported a higher rate of drug use by family members than did students districtwide. This confirms the program's assumption that family mental health interventions are a requirement early in the student's life to establish an effective environment for the student's positive development. Students need assistance early on in dealing with the damaging elements prevalent in their environment if they are to avoid the pitfalls presented by early and frequent acquaintance with drug abuse, family violence, and family disruption.

Program Development During the 1990–91 School Year

Four major School of the Future programs have been initiated at J.T. Brackenridge during the 1990–91 school year in support of family mental health. Research has also been completed in preparation for a fifth program, Children's Creative Response to Conflict (CCRC). A core group of faculty received training on how to implement these programs. The first year's primary goal was the provision of programs addressing family concerns and encouraging parents to join the school as part of their children's education team. These programs are never static. Modification of ongoing programs and the addition of new programs will continue as parents, children, and faculty discover other needs which can be addressed through a cooperative effort.

The four new programs installed in the first year and continued into the second were the following:

1. Family, individual, and group therapy;
2. Advocacy and education concerning social services;
3. Parent education; and
4. Development of a parent volunteer core.

During the second year the following programs are being added:

1. Programs such as CCRC that provide alternatives to violence;
2. Use of outside volunteers to provide expanded support services;
3. Increased participation of parents and students in school management; and
4. Expanded involvement of private corporations in the program.

A brief description of the four programs already well established follows.

Family, Individual, and Group Therapy. Our Lady of the Lake University, St. Mary's University, and The University of Texas at San Antonio all agreed to the placement of master's level interns at J.T. Brackenridge. By the end of the 1990–91 school year, five interns had provided therapy for families and family members at J.T. In the past, families and students had been referred to outside facilities, but they often could not follow through due to lack of transportation, lack of child care, or misunderstanding of how therapy could assist them in their situation. Therapy groups for students began during the second semester at the school to assist children in the sharing of similar problems. The project initially offered two groups, one for fourth graders and one for kindergartners and first and second graders. At least six groups will be offered during the second year.

During the initial two semesters of operation, the Family Support Program provided 824 hours of therapy distributed over the following areas: individual sessions with student or parent (472 hours), family sessions (329 hours), and group sessions (23 hours). While referral initially came from teachers and counselors at the school, during the second semester the project saw an increase in self-referrals and "walk-ins" who became aware of the services through their neighbors and friends. The program experienced a 75 percent attendance rate, with "no-shows" and cancellations decreasing during the second semester as families became accustomed to their counseling schedule, and therapists established rapport with them.

Eighty-six students and/or their families were actively involved in therapy (seen three or more times) during this past year. Presenting problems, while varied, tended to cluster in specific behavior areas. Numerous additional areas became apparent as the counseling process continued (see Table 1).

Table 1

Most Frequently Presented Problems for 86 Families
After at Least Three Counseling Sessions

Children's problems as identified by parent or teacher

Behavior problems	31
Aggressive physical behavior	8
Depression or withdrawal	7
Sexual abuse	5
Enuresis (involuntary urination)	5
Physical abuse	4
Inappropriate sex, theft, grief resolution, poor hygiene, abandonment, anxiety	2 each

Parents' problems as identified by parent

Alcohol/drug dependency	19
Marital/relationship discord	18
Poor parenting skills	18
Neglect in parenting	8
Anxiety	8
Physical abuse	8
Depression	3
Schizophrenia	3
Rape	2
Sexual abuse	2

One case seen this year typifies the positive movement possible when families are given the opportunity to identify clearly their alternatives for change. A family of six, two inhalant-abusing parents and four boys, was referred by the school nurse for counseling due to medical neglect. The father had already experienced some brain damage due to substance abuse; the mother was guarded and distant in her approach to outsiders, as well as to family members; and the children fluctuated between withdrawn, passive behavior and "acting out" in class. After five months of intensive therapy with the mother and children, the mother remained sober. She has developed parenting strategies for her children and explored the alternatives for dealing with her spouse, who continues his substance abuse.

A common problem seen in therapy with parents who started having children as teenagers is their lack of positive parenting skills. They also have difficulty with adult relationships and problems in setting long-term goals. They feel out of control as parents when their once normal children become "crazy" upon reaching puberty. Parents do not know how to deal with rearing a teenager when they themselves never experienced being a teen, just a teen parent. As a result, their children often adopt the same "script" as did their parents when they, in turn, become adults. Material gathered in the household surveys indicates that approximately 30 percent of the mothers with children enrolled at J.T. Brackenridge gave birth at age 17 or younger.

Advocacy and Education Concerning Social Services. The Worden School of Social Service, Our Lady of the Lake University, agreed to the placement of practicum students at the J.T. Brackenridge campus. The social work interns provided 276 hours of service to clients during the spring semester. Specific services provided were crisis intervention, counseling, advocacy work for clients with agencies, Child Protective Service (CPS) referrals, and a variety of other supportive assistance. The primary goal throughout the semester was to assure that students and their families obtain the services needed to build a stable home environment.

During the first year, several CPS caseworkers made direct referrals to the program and participated in some of the family therapy sessions at the school. In an effort to assure more continuity and follow-up, two CPS workers are being designated in the second year to screen all of the reports coming to their facility which concern J.T. families.

The first CPS case involved four children in "the care" of their 90-year-old great-grandmother. The oldest child, a 13-year-old female, had dropped out of school and was working the streets as a prostitute. Her brothers cared for their great-grandmother. They often came to school without clean clothes or food. The program staff contacted the local family court judge and assisted in having the children placed in a stable environment.

This instance illustrates the kind of situation where intervention physically separates members of a family. Sometimes family problems are so extreme that solutions require removing some family members from the environment and securing for them a new situation with a stronger support system. The necessity for occasional interventions of this nature can increase the anxiety with which other families approach the School of the Future project, feeding their fears that their children might be removed, a potentially negative side effect that must be considered.

Parent Education. Parent education sessions were conducted throughout the school year to aid parents in developing skills to assist their own healthy development as well as their children's. Formal presentations were made mostly through the Parent Education Program, City of San Antonio. The final presentation, "How to Talk with My Child's Teacher," was led by two J.T. faculty members.

The project is exploring ways to provide more education sessions during evening hours as well as school hours in order to reach more parents. Parent volunteers assisted in getting the word out about parent education programs by phoning other parents. Additional parent networking and incentives to increase attendance are being employed in the second year.

A directory of local services was compiled at the end of the first year for distribution to all parents. Work on the directory started at the beginning of the school year and was completed by a Brown University Fellow in summer placement at J.T. The directory should assist parents in identifying needed services within the community and will help in educating families about how to obtain these services.

Development of a Parent Volunteer Core. Parents were recruited as volunteers at the school in order to develop better self-esteem, to become invested in their children's education, and to develop basic job skills for themselves. Training offered by the program assisted parents in undertaking new tasks and gave them confidence to take leadership roles in the school. A core of parents emerged who encouraged other neighbors and friends, through phone calls and personal contact, to become involved in the education and volunteer programs.

In order to provide a foundation and understanding of what would be expected of a parent volunteer, 16 meetings were held during the year with parent volunteers. These meetings were held weekly during the first semester and every other week during the second semester. The meetings focused on basic job expectations (sign-in, appropriate dress, etc.), communicating with school personnel and children, and problem resolution. The group decided that it would be helpful if parents could be readily identified as volunteers by other school personnel. Parents sewed blue and gold aprons for women and vests for men to wear when on duty. Volunteers assisted as classroom assistants, cafeteria monitors, office assistants, library aides, and general office assistants. Due to a request from the second grade teachers, a computer lab was opened for their students, totally staffed and overseen by the parent volunteers during the second semester.

Children's Creative Response to Conflict. In response to referrals from parents and faculty to children's discipline and behavioral problems, a search was conducted to locate a school-based program which could assist in establishing a safe, educational environment for learning. The Children's Creative Response to Conflict program was selected as a viable vehicle for assisting the faculty in this task.

Since 1972, the CCRC program has been training faculty and students in all areas of the country in learning alternative ways to deal with conflict in school and in their community. The program has four core elements: cooperation, communication, affirmation, and conflict resolution. A 30-hour training session was held midway through the first year for 12 volunteer faculty members. Trainers assisted these faculty members in learning the techniques, as well as in how to train other faculty. At the beginning of the second year this core group has been training the entire faculty, as well as classroom assistants, librarians, and clerical staff, so that these techniques can be implemented with the start of the school year. This program will inform all students that they often have numerous options from which to choose when facing conflicts.

Areas for Development During the Second Year

With the experience of the first year and increased research data on the community, project staff have planned several extensions of the program for the second academic year.

Use of Outside Volunteers to Provide Expanded Support Services. Thirty church volunteers—currently undergoing orientation to the project— are staffing the expansion of social services. Volunteers serve as parenting mentors, tutors, literacy instructors for parents, and child care providers.

Increased Parent and Student Management Participation. An active school management team was in place by September 1991. The initial year focused on providing programs requested by families. Through this first year's activities, parents became associated with the new program and identified other parents who could serve as part of a cooperative management team. The team is beginning to carry responsibility for such programs as parent education.

Expanded Corporate Involvement in the Program. HEB Food Company, a large retail grocery chain headquartered in San Antonio, adopted the San Antonio School of the Future and is the primary corporate sponsor. It has provided $20,000 toward second-year operations, as well as the purchase and installation of a satellite dish antenna for educational programming. While effort will continue in order to attract additional business and foundation support, it will be done with the understanding that the project must be kept cost-efficient if it is ever to be duplicated or expanded in the future.

Conclusion

This overview of the San Antonio School of the Future project opened with a view from the media of the turmoil associated with the housing project. Children and their families experience daily problems with extreme poverty, violence, drug addiction, and abandonment. However, the demography of the community is as much an indictment of society's lack of response as of the neighborhood itself.

During the first year, above all else, the School of the Future staff discovered the strong sense of dignity parents possess and their willingness to work for better opportunities for their children. In spite of numerous financial, environmental, and bureaucratic obstacles, parents working as volunteers, families taking risks in therapy, and parents sharing their thoughts frankly with instructors and administrators have provided the basis for creating an environment which reinforces positive mental health for individuals and families.

As parents become more involved and self-confident in participating in their children's education, however, the faculty take on additional burdens. As in therapy, when change takes place, stress on the system increases before it lessens. The ability of the school staff to work together with families, as opposed to being in an adversarial position, will determine the eventual success of the project.

The struggle for change and the optimism seen in these families are expressed poignantly in a note written by the inhalant-abusing mother described earlier. Addressed to her therapist, the note (presented here as she wrote it) demonstrates not only gratitude for his assistance, but the hope for a fuller life for herself:

> To my wise friend who thought me how to overcome several problems. When I first started attending these sessisons I was fearful of this stranger whom I felt was inviding my privite live. I begin to built this defensive wall around me in order not to let you know what was behind it. Through several sessions, feelings of anger, resentment, guilt, embarrament and mistrust were let out and in it's place came an understanding that indeed this person honsently seemed to care about me as a person. You helped me realize that we all need help and that you were not being judgementle. You took this person as was and brought out the best in me. I thank God for sending you to me, as I feel I can overcome almost any obstable that get's in my way. I feel stronger and less burdened and I have you and God to thank you for changing my life for the better! God Bless You Alway's....

Supportive, creative, self-directed school-based programs are needed if families from public housing projects are to gain an equal opportunity for growth and self-determination. The School of the Future must become a reality—today—before another generation of potential becomes lost within the walls of projects like the Alazan/Apache Courts.

References

Lein, L. (1990). Proposal to the Rockefeller Foundation.
Lein, L. (1991). *The role of food programs in the lives of persistently poor children.* Manuscript in preparation.
San Antonio Cares. (1990). Personal communication.
Tobin, Richard. (1990). Personal communication.

CHAPTER 7

A Declaration of Beliefs and Visions:
Houston's School of the Future

by

Hugh F. Crean & Harriet Arvey

The concept of expanding the school experience beyond the processes of learning through the provision of essential human/supportive services within the school setting is not new in Houston. The predominantly Hispanic-populated Hogg Middle School has been the site of several successful efforts demonstrating the value of attending in an integrated manner to the complex child and family problems that are obstacles to effective learning and growth. This infusion of "nontraditional" approaches and resources into the Hogg Middle School and neighborhood has provided an excellent platform from which to chart Houston's School of the Future.

Background in Houston

Beginning with the 1987–88 school year the Family Service Center (FSC) of Houston, a nonprofit counseling and educational service center, opened an outreach family counseling office at Hogg Middle School. With ongoing support from the school principal, the Family Service Center's presence has been augmented with an increasing array of supportive volunteer and organizational programming. Each individual volunteer and organizational entity has provided an essential service for the children and families living in an otherwise underserved area. The following four programs were already present within the neighborhood when the School of the Future was established and continue to be active at the Hogg Middle School.

The Metropolitan Organization (TMO) has been actively involved with the Hogg Middle School community for the past four years. TMO is a community advocacy organization whose main thrust is to empower the neighborhood parents to become more effective social advocates on behalf of services needed. They have also been working with the school and the parents to make the neighborhood a stronger and safer area.

The Multi-Ethnic Cultural Association (MECA) provides a variety of support services for the Hispanic population, specifically targeting youth activities both during the school year and in the summer. MECA is an association affiliated with St. Joseph's Roman Catholic Church and works with the youth in numerous arts activities such as putting on plays, talent shows, painting, and writing.

Dispute Resolution Services, a new program of the Harris County District Court, teaches Hogg Middle School youth alternatives to violence in settling conflict in their lives. Many children already have a history of school discipline problems, including a number of incidents of students fighting with each other or student violence toward teachers. Violence is often the only option considered by many of these students. By providing youth with creative options other than violence, this program has significantly reduced the number of aggressive incidents in the school.

Coopers and Lybrand, a major accounting firm in Houston, had adopted Hogg Middle School as a site for volunteer tutoring. The firm gives its employees time off to work with individual students who have special educational needs. In addition, the firm provides cash grants to the school based upon the number of volunteer hours given by their employees. Their involvement has improved the academic achievement of the students in this program.

The above efforts are individually and collectively commendable, and demonstrate that an initial thrust at changing traditional approaches within the school can be sustained, gaining momentum through the increased involvement of a greater number of individuals and organizations. As volunteers and professionals alike have been witness to the initial successes of a "new experience" within the school, their enthusiasm has been contagious.

The School of the Future project affords Houston an excellent opportunity for further demonstration of this active partnership in the application of neighborhood-based, integrated public education and community services.

Guiding Principles of the Houston School of the Future

These experiences of the past several years have led to a shared set of beliefs among a variety of individuals and organizations associated with Houston's Hogg Middle School. These shared beliefs were experienced but went mostly unspoken until the opportunity was presented by the Hogg Foundation to come together for reflection and planning associated with the

School of the Future project. This reflection and planning has produced the following shared beliefs that are seen as essential for a successful family, school, and community partnership:

- The family, neighborhood school, and community service resources available to serve the developmental needs of children must come together as a working system if they are to be responsive and effective in addressing the challenges for optimal development of these children.
- The problems and issues confronting developmental success for the children and families of the neighborhood are complex, requiring innovative approaches and multiple educational, health, and human services.
- The resources of the family, school, and community will only work as a fully functioning system if all components of the system are involved together in identifying issues and solving problems.
- The involvement of families, school personnel, and a variety of community service professionals and volunteers will take place only to the extent that each believes they belong to a working "partnership"—a relationship involving close cooperation between parties having specified and joint rights and responsibilities, a partnership with the expressed purpose of facilitating change.
- The neighborhood and school is the philosophical and practical focus for this partnership, while also recognizing that the school cannot succeed alone.
- The predominance of a growing Hispanic population in the neighborhood and school dictates indigenous participation in the partnership, including a preference for bilingual, bicultural capacity in project coordination.
- Training for school and community service resource personnel in the principles of family dynamics and the practices of healthy family functioning is an essential component of long-term system development.
- The infrastructure of the project must be minimally formal and maximally flexible.

To aid in this flexibility, the Family Service Center in Houston serves as the grant recipient and fiscal manager of the project, a different plan from the other three School of the Future sites. As fiscal manager, the Family Service Center provides the advantages of flexibility and easy access to the use of these funds, avoiding the bureaucracy and problems inherent in the administration of a large school district.

The Needs

Three schools in an area known as "the Heights" form the nucleus of Houston's School of the Future—Hogg Middle School, Memorial Elementary, and Brock Elementary. The Heights is part of the Houston Independent School District XII and lies northwest of downtown Houston. It is a mostly Hispanic area and very poor. Like many inner-city neighborhoods, violence, drug abuse, poverty, child neglect, and other social ills are all evident in the Heights. Such environments have a profound effect on children. Results from two needs assessments conducted early in the development of the School of the Future confirmed these beliefs and highlighted many of the needs of these children and their families.

Family Assessment Interviews. As an early part of the project, the project coordinator identified and interviewed 45 adults from 30 families who were already receiving services from the Hogg Middle School Counseling Program. The demographics of these families are striking. None of the adults interviewed had permanent employment. The average income of these families was less than $12,000 per year. Less than 10 percent of the parents spoke any English. Half were single-parent families. Over half of the families interviewed had at least four children in the school-aged years. Figure 1 illustrates graphically the problems identified by these families.

Although obtained from a nonrandom sample, the information provided illustrates the difficulties these families have in meeting basic needs as well as the multifaceted nature of the problems faced. The problems identified fall into two areas, the family and the school. These problems occur in a family environment dominated by substance abuse and emotional deprivation. The school then finds itself dealing with the negative manifestations of this home environment, behaviors impacting not only the education of the individual student but also the educational environment of the school.

Youth Risk Behavior Surveys of Fifth and Eighth Grade Students. In the fall of 1991 the Center for Disease Control's Youth Risk Behavior Survey was administered to the eighth graders of the Hogg Middle School. The survey elicited data on six priority health-risk behaviors: (1) behaviors that result in intentional and unintentional injuries; (2) drug and alcohol use; (3) tobacco use; (4) sexual behaviors that result in HIV infection, other sexually transmitted diseases, and unintended pregnancies; (5) dietary behaviors

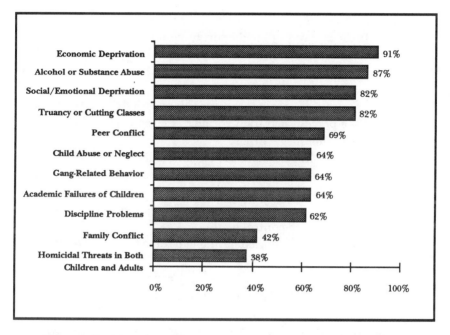

Figure 1. Problems identified by Family Assessment Interviews of those receiving Hogg Middle School counseling services ($n = 45$).

and (6) physical activity. Of these, the first four are of primary concern although the benefits of good dietary behavior and physical activity are also recognized. Two-hundred thirty-nine students completed the survey out of a possible 293—128 girls and 111 boys. The results present cause for concern. Especially relevant were the following findings:

- In the 30 days prior to the administration of the survey, 43 percent of the boys and 20 percent of the girls had some form of weapon at school or in the neighborhood. Knives were the most frequent weapon (16%), followed by guns (9%).
- Fifty-five percent of the eighth grade students had been in a physical fight within the past 12 months with 8 percent having been in six or more fights in that time period. Four percent were with more than one person.
- Roughly 27 percent of the students had considered suicide in the past year with 20 percent making at least one behavioral suicide attempt.
- Eleven percent of these students admitted to smoking cigarettes

regularly, 2 percent smoking more than five cigarettes per day.

- In the 30 days prior to the survey's administration, 46 percent of the students sampled had had at least one alcoholic drink. Five percent of those who drank had had at least one drink on 20 or more of those 30 days.

- Twenty-two percent of the students had tried or used marijuana. Nine percent had tried cocaine. Eleven percent had used or tried other illegal drugs.

- Thirty-eight percent of the eighth graders reported experiencing sexual intercourse (54 percent of the boys and 24 percent of the girls). Of students who reported having intercourse, 62 percent had multiple partners. Thirty-three percent reported using no birth control method.

- Four percent reported having had some form of sexually transmitted disease.

- Ten students reported getting pregnant or getting someone pregnant while another five were unsure if pregnancy had occurred.

A survey of health-risk behaviors was also given to the fifth graders at the two elementary schools in the project, Brock and Memorial. The survey elicited data on household demographics, drug and alcohol use, and tobacco use. One hundred nine students (63 boys and 46 girls) completed the survey out of a possible 121. Some of the more pertinent results follow:

- Most children's households had six or more people in the home (55 percent), 10 percent had three or less.

- Sixty-three percent of the fifth graders had had more than a sip of alcohol; 24 percent claimed five or more times.

- Sixty-one percent of the students had never smoked more than a puff of a cigarette, 16 percent had smoked more than a puff five or more times. Forty-nine percent had friends who smoked.

- Fifteen percent of fifth graders reported having used marijuana; 8 percent five or more times. Ten percent had four or more friends using marijuana. Twenty percent reported a lot of pressure from their friends to use marijuana; 65 percent reported no pressure.

- Seventy-three percent reported having seen someone selling drugs in their neighborhood; 9 percent involving a family member. Fifty-two percent had seen someone smoking crack cocaine; 11 percent of these students had been asked to sell crack cocaine.

Results from these surveys will be used to target interventions. Such data have already provided the needed documentation to obtain grants and other available resources.

Participating Schools

Hogg Middle School, Memorial Elementary, and Brock Elementary are all participating in the Houston School of the Future project. A situation unique to the Houston site is that the schools are located in three distinct neighborhoods, making coordination more difficult. Both elementary schools feed into Hogg Middle School.

Each of these schools has a new principal who is very committed to the project and has become quite active in obtaining needed resources for the school. This commitment has resulted in similar enthusiasm and support being seen in the teaching staff at each of the schools. Like the School of the Future site in San Antonio, these schools are often seen as a haven for these children. The three schools have excellent attendance records. Table 1 presents the student characteristics of each of the schools.

Hogg Middle School. The Hogg Middle School serves grades 6 through 8. It is a growing school. The student population has increased significantly since last year. There are now close to 1,100 students in the school, 89 percent of whom are Hispanic. Three quarters of the children qualify for the federal free or reduced lunch program and more than 30 percent are from single-parent homes. Half the children are overage for their class.

As previously discussed, Hogg Middle School already had a variety of counseling and tutoring programs before the School of the Future project was started. Other, more recently implemented programs, have also been active. For example, the Gulf Coast Alliance for Minorities in Education (GCAME) program sponsors 25 engineers from the Shell-Western Corporation to help eighth grade students in a math or science project. Each volunteer also becomes a mentor for a student, assisting in developing a plan for the student's future in high school and beyond.

Another mentoring program available to many students at Hogg is Leadership 2000. A group of 25 predominantly Hispanic lawyers talk to different groups of students about how they worked to become successful. Many of the lawyers share backgrounds similar to the students at Hogg Middle School, a few having grown up in the same neighborhood. These volunteers also offer individualized career planning for students.

The Family Service Center counseling program has now become an integral part of the school. The counselor in the program provides students

Table 1

Student Characteristics of the Three Participating Schools for the 1990 School Year

	Hogg Middle School	Brock Elementary	Memorial Elementary
Number of students	1,065	307	419
Grades	6 to 8	Pre-K to 6	Pre-K to 5
Ethnicity			
% African-American	7	30	3
% Hispanic	89	69	93
% non-Hispanic white	3	1	4
% other	<1	<1	<1
Economic			
% free lunch program	68	95	82
% reduced lunch program	7	4	8
Special population			
% special education	17	13	3
% limited English program	41	40	54
Attendance percentage	92.5	95.3	97.2

Source: Houston Independent School District, Research and Evaluation Department. (1991). *HISD District and School Profiles, 1990–91.* Houston: Author.

and their families with a variety of programs and services dealing with substance abuse, child abuse, school dropout, teen pregnancy, and suicide. They also link families with other community agencies and programs when appropriate. A number of teachers interviewed in the Key Informant Surveys not only praised the effectiveness of the counselors with the students and families, but also commented on how easy and natural it was to refer students to the program and to interact with the counselors.

Another positive development at the school is the recent hiring of a Hispanic principal as well as the hiring of more bilingual teachers. While the proportion of Hispanic teachers has been growing, the school's teaching staff is still only 8 percent Hispanic. In a school whose students are 89 percent Hispanic, the hiring of more Hispanic staff was urgently needed and has quickly improved the communication between teachers, students, and parents.

A major issue as the School of the Future started in Houston was the community's perception of the school. Racial tensions, gang activity, and drug problems were all perceived to be "running rampant." Much of this reputation stemmed from an incident which occurred five years earlier. Students from a nearby high school gathered to watch a fight between a high school student and one of the older middle school students. Other middle school students were also watching. The groups provoked each other with racial insults. Violence broke out. Police were eventually called in to break up the incident which made local TV news, where many of the parents witnessed the event. Although no such incident has occurred since, this memory continues to linger in the community.

This negative community image is a primary concern for the principal and many of the project staff. It affects the student body, as many parents elect to send their children to magnet schools or private schools rather than to Hogg Middle School, even though many of these children have expressed a desire to be with friends at the neighborhood school. The situation is improving now that the principal has targeted the community's perception as an immediate concern. For example, the guidance counselors visited and presented information about the middle school to the fifth grade students of its 13 elementary feeder schools. Parents were also invited to attend. Although the counselors found that rumors still existed, they were no longer badly exaggerated. Most of the students, teachers, and parents in the 13 schools reported hearing good things about the middle school, particularly in regard to its academic program and the social services offered. For example, in talking with a Brock Elementary teacher, it was learned that a family was debating whether to have their daughter attend one of Houston's magnet schools or the Hogg Middle School. The parents and daughter were so impressed by this presentation and the warmth of the guidance counselors that she and her family immediately decided that Hogg was the best school for her. Nevertheless, many families continue to send their children to other schools without considering all the available options.

The principal and staff feel that merely getting parents into the school can influence this perception. Since many of the parents in this neighborhood are intimidated by the school, a first step must be to make parents comfortable about being in the school. Many staff members felt that more positive incentives were needed for parents to visit the school. One teacher discussed creating a "Jazzercise" class for parents and teachers, allowing for more informal and natural interaction. Once parents feel at home in the school, a stronger Parent-Teacher Organization (PTO) can be formed. In the first year of the project there were a few faithful PTO members, but these were all parents of eighth graders who were graduating.

A critical need in the neighborhood is to have more activities for children, a theme common to all three participating schools. There are no organized places to play other than the school yard. Organized activities for children are almost nonexistent. There is much unsupervised time; students are out of school by 3:15 p.m. while their parents work until 5:00 or 6:00 most evenings. Many parents and teachers have expressed a need for more after-school recreation with adult supervision. The possibility exists for Hogg Middle School and other service providers to offer a variety of summer and after-school programs for students.

Another concern common to all three schools is the families' reliance solely upon the school nurse for medical care. There are no accessible clinics or other health care providers in these neighborhoods, the nearest clinic is a 20-minute drive. Because of triage, families must often wait hours at the clinic before being seen. In addition, many families are intimidated by these clinics since they are not yet residents of this country and fear legal action being taken against them.

Memorial Elementary School. Memorial Elementary, built during the 1920s, has a student population of just over 400. Planned renovations over the next six months will bring another 100 children to the school. Although the school sits adjacent to Memorial Park, the school's student population comes from an extremely poor neighborhood isolated from the park by a major thoroughfare. Houses in the neighborhood lack screens on doors, windows are often broken, and rarely do any of these houses have air conditioning. Over half of the elementary-aged students at Memorial are home alone or with siblings at some point during the day. Health and human services are nonexistent in the neighborhood.

Although poor, the neighborhood is a stable one with most families having lived here for more than 10 years. The teachers at Memorial know the neighborhood and its families, facilitating school/home interactions. Many teachers have been to these students' homes. If a phone is available in the home, teachers will call parents regularly to keep them informed of their child's progress. Knowing what's going on in these children's homes has allowed teachers to be more sensitive to the many needs of their students.

Many families have come to rely on teachers as consultants for a number of services. For example, some teachers filled out tax returns for families last year, and teachers have developed a form letter for families to use as proof of residence. The school accepts responsibility for assisting these families. Teachers are very much aware of their role as social service brokers and have asked for help since they are often unaware of available services or how to access them. They share many of the same fears experienced by the families in dealing with the large, centralized bureaucracies of Houston.

Organized parent involvement at Memorial was virtually nonexistent in past years. An active and committed Parent-Teacher Organization was seen by many of the teaching staff as the biggest need at Memorial. Last year the active PTO consisted of one person working single-handedly to organize and run the "organization." When this person became employed at the school and was no longer able to continue in her role as PTO president, the PTO vanished. Given the amount of communication that occurs between the school and home, the teachers at Memorial were unsure as to why the school was unable to organize a PTO, but they are determined to succeed.

At Memorial, there is a good mix of experience among the 22 teachers, four or five having been there for more than 15 years while three or four are in their first year teaching. The concept of teachers working as a team is fundamental to Memorial's view of education. Communication is open and teachers have input into all educational issues. They are not afraid to ask for advice nor to give or receive constructive criticism.

Resources at Memorial have been quite limited. The only school/business partner involved with the school prior to the onset of the School of the Future project was International Business Machines (IBM), which had several volunteers active in providing math and science training. The company has also provided cash awards to the school as well as the donation of a number of IBM personal computers. Physical resources are also limited at Memorial. Space at the school is extremely scarce, somewhat constraining the amount of volunteer involvement during the school day. Four of the six key informant surveys conducted at the school were held either in the hallways or in the cafeteria. Teaching assistants must use the area behind the cafeteria stage as office space. Despite such difficulties, Memorial has a good academic program. On the latest standardized testing the school ranked fifteenth out of 90 schools in the Houston Independent School District—an excellent accomplishment given the school's socioeconomic makeup and the difficulties with language encountered by many of the students.

The elementary teachers are particularly concerned with the need to focus educational goals as a united group of teaching professionals, not just as three separate levels of teachers (elementary, middle, and high school). Although dropout is a problem seen in high schools and some middle schools, the elementary schools have equal responsibility and cannot be excluded in working toward a solution. Many of the teachers were excited by the possibilities created by the School of the Future for addressing such issues in a systematic way.

Brock Elementary School. Brock Elementary has just 307 students in kindergarten through sixth grade. The neighborhood is highly transitional; as little as 15 years ago, African-Americans made up the predominant population. Today the neighborhood is 70 percent Hispanic. The school is located on one of Houston's major streets and is surrounded by small businesses and run-down cantinas. It is a high-crime area.

The school is often described as "the nicest building in the neighborhood." Unlike Memorial, it is a relatively new school with plenty of physical resources to serve its students. The children and families of the neighborhood use the school grounds for recreation. Other than the school the only social service resources in the neighborhood are the churches. The school and churches often must work together with parents in solving neighborhood crises. Other than the school playground there are no accessible recreation areas for the children. A freeway must be crossed to reach the nearest park. More structured recreation is badly needed. The only organized sports in the area are sponsored by the YMCA located two miles away. Children in this neighborhood are forced to wait until middle school before starting Little League or other athletics. By then, the level of competition is too intense for youth just starting out. Boys and girls interested in the arts also must wait until middle school and then must usually go to a more remote magnet school to get advanced training.

The teaching staff at Brock is young and enthusiastic, two-thirds of the 15 instructors having less than three years' experience. Many were impressed with each other's focus on social problems and awareness of the needs of their students. A number also commented favorably on the staff's detailed knowledge of the limited resources available to families and knowledge of the informal networks in the neighborhood. Staff morale is very good.

Brock's current business partners include volunteers from Apple Computer, Southwestern Bell Telephone, and Winstead, Sechrest, and Minick, a local law firm. Representatives from such industries as well as teachers and parents make up Brock's Private Sector Initiative Council, which has provided the school with a cash grant of $1,500 to sponsor parental involvement activities this past year. These companies also provide a variety of mentoring and tutoring programs. For example, lawyers give tutoring in the social sciences and sponsor a yearly "mock court" experience.

St. Joseph's Multi-Ethnic Cultural Association is also quite active at Brock Elementary, sponsoring an after-school and summer arts program available for local students. The group also provides professional artists, writers, and actors who voluntarily spend one morning per week with interested students. In the spring of 1991 the actor in residence worked with students in producing a play for the parents of Brock.

As with Memorial and Hogg schools, staff at Brock believe that parental involvement in school governance is critical to the success of the school. Parents feel better about being in the school as a result of the "Parents as Partners" program and the Chapter 1 Morning Meetings. The "Parents as Partners" program was devised specifically for attracting parents into the school. Using the grant of $1,500 from the Private Sector Initiative Council, the staff sponsored bimonthly evening meetings at the school for parents and teachers. Each meeting covered a different topic as suggested by the parents, providing a forum for speakers from different agencies to discuss their programs or ideas. Dinner was served buffet style at the school, and child care was provided by volunteer teachers who showed a movie or provided other forms of organized entertainment. From 80 to 100 families came to each meeting. A core group of fourth-grade parents who can serve as future PTO leaders has been identified by their participation in this program.

Parents have also been brought more closely into the school by a program known as the Chapter 1 Morning Meetings. Monthly meetings are coordinated by the Chapter 1 counselor focusing on basic parenting skills. The program takes a developmental approach, dealing with the capabilities of children at different life stages. Speakers from local human service agencies are also brought in to discuss available free or low-cost services. Starting with only 4 mothers in January 1991, the group had 16 mothers and 2 fathers by May. Although Brock Elementary has done reasonably well in developing these programs, more parent involvement in the governing of the school is needed.

Project Goals

The above information presents some of the existing strengths and needs at each of the schools. The programming in place prior to the project's onset was certainly seen as an asset to these schools and to the project staff. Nevertheless, such programs must be supplemented and urgent needs properly addressed if the School of the Future is to achieve its overall goal of enhancing the physical, emotional, intellectual, and behavioral development of these neighborhood children.

In Houston, three broadly defined objectives must first be met before the realization of the project's goals will occur. These specified objectives are (1) to increase and to improve the quality of parental involvement at each school; (2) to obtain needed resources for the children; and (3) to coordinate resources such that service delivery occurs in a smooth and naturalistic manner. Success of the School of the Future lies in the amount of ownership of the project assumed by the neighborhood parents. Since many of these parents are uncomfortable at the school, work 10–14 hours per day, and are single parents rearing several children, involving them must be well thought out and done with patience. With some mechanisms already in place, the project staff is optimistic about increasing the level of parental involvement in the project.

Basic resources such as health care, recreational facilities, and social services are lacking in these schools and neighborhoods. In one school the physical space to involve parents, volunteers, and other services during the school day is limited. Accessible resources must be available, and delivery of such resources must occur in a smooth manner. Any new services that are implemented should not become an extra bureaucratic layer for families to negotiate or for the school personnel to administer. Services must be integrated and must complement the existing ecology of the schools and neighborhood.

Organization of Houston's School of the Future

The Houston School of the Future project is guided through the knowledge, advice, and involvement of the project coordinator, the Partnership Council, and the Partnership Council's executive committee.

The Project Coordinator. The project coordinator is central to the development of the School of the Future. Qualifications for the position include the following: (1) knowledge and experience in working with individuals, groups, and community organizations; (2) knowledge of community service resources; (3) knowledge and understanding of the importance of advocacy in promoting community/systems change; (4) knowledge and understanding of the Hispanic population, its culture, and its community, with bilingual capability preferred; and (5) understanding of and commitment to the necessity of changing traditional approaches to public education and family/school/community resource integration.

The project coordinator is responsible for bringing together the various services at each school as well as for keeping the records for research and monitoring of the project. A bilingual, Hispanic social worker serves as coordinator bringing to the program an extensive knowledge of community organization and development. He has past experience working with the Houston schools in various capacities including direct services, planning, and administration. The coordinator has oriented each school's principal, staff, and parents to the concept of the program. In addition, he has been working to organize a Parent Council at each school to be involved in the governance of the project. The project coordinator has also helped secure needed business and community "partners" for each school.

The Partnership Council. The Partnership Council was designed to allow systematic input to the program from the view of the direct service provider as well as to open the lines of communication among the various service agencies. Initially, current service agencies already in place at the schools were given the opportunity to provide representation. Thus, the Partnership Council includes representatives from the following: Coopers & Lybrand Accounting Firm; the Harris County Court Services; the Family Service Center; GCAME Shell-Western; IBM; Leadership 2000; The Metropolitan Organization (TMO); Apple Computer; St. Joseph's Multi-Ethnic Cultural Association; The University of Texas Health Science Center at Houston's School of Public Health; and the law firm of Winstead, Sechrest, & Minick. Others on the Council are drawn from the parents and school staff. As new service providers involve themselves in the project, they are also given the opportunity to appoint representatives to the council.

The Executive Committee. Direct governance of the School of the Future in Houston rests with the executive committee of the Partnership Council. Among their responsibilities are the defining of local objectives for the project, the procurement of needed resources and partners, and overseeing the activities of the project coordinator. The executive committee, consisting of 12 members from Houston's Partnership Council, represents parents, key service providers, school and educational personnel, and the private sector. A designated administrator from the Houston Independent School District serves as chair of the executive committee while a representative from the Family Service Center serves as vice-chair. The principals from the three schools serve on the executive committee as does one parent member. The project coordinator is an ex-officio member of the executive committee.

Accomplishments of the Past Year

A number of major accomplishments have been achieved in the past year. For example, in each of the three schools a Parent Council has been established to facilitate communication between the school staff and the neighborhood families. These councils meet several times throughout the school year and provide input to the project coordinator, the three principals, and the executive committee. Selected parents from these councils have also received training from the United Way in how to use Houston's Help Line. The parents are taught how to use a variety of human service resources, information they give to the neighborhood families. These trained parents are reimbursed for the services they render, giving them special leadership status in the community.

At Hogg Middle School more than 200 students and their families received counseling from the Family Service Center's Hogg Counseling Project. The services dealt with substance abuse, child abuse, school dropout, teen pregnancy, and suicide. Families were also referred to other community agencies and programs when appropriate. During the past school year demands of the program necessitated the hiring of another counselor, who also works full-time at the school. The Family Service Center has also received funding from the Texas Commission on Alcohol and Drug Abuse to provide specialized treatment services for the chemically dependent, marginal-income Hispanic adults in the School of the Future neighborhoods. In addition, the Multi-Ethnic Cultural Association also plans to fund counseling services for youth at Hogg Middle School who are in danger of leaving school and becoming involved in Houston's drug culture. "Kick Drugs Out of America," a program developed by Chuck Norris, will also be active in the second year. This program focuses on staying off drugs while also teaching students karate skills.

The Hogg Middle School is also offering an accelerated academic program to its sixth grade students, the SIGHTS (Supplemental Instruction for Gifted, High Achieving and/or Talented Students). Previously offered only at the elementary level, the program is being piloted in four sixth-grade classrooms with plans to expand the program to grades seven and eight in the next two years. The SIGHTS classes aid youngsters whose scores on standardized tests, grades, and teacher recommendations indicate that they would benefit from a more accelerated and challenging curriculum. The program is expected to have a positive effect on the entire school body by attracting young leaders who can serve as role models for other students. Brock Elementary School sixth graders are also participating in the SIGHTS program.

At Memorial Elementary a part-time clinical psychology intern assisted by providing counseling services to more than 35 parents and their children. A direct outgrowth of this service has been Laurelwood Psychiatric Hospital's offering of Hispanic therapists to conduct family support classes in the second year. A Girl Scout Activity Center has also been started at Memorial. Nearly 50 girls participate in the program at no cost to themselves or their parents. A parental component has been planned for the second year. The MECA program has also expanded to include Memorial Elementary in its provision of arts and cultural services.

The Houston Independent School District has increased the ancillary staffing at both elementary schools, providing each with a full-time nurse and a half-time counselor. At Brock Elementary this has allowed the principal to use Chapter 1 funds to develop an after-school program focusing on esteem development and physical activity. The program is offered by the local YMCA, which provides two counselors who structure after-school activities for the children. In addition, the Houston Police Department's DARE program has provided drug education prevention services to Brock Elementary fifth grade students.

Recently, the Houston Apartment Association and the Houston Independent School District's STAY program have begun collaborating to reduce student/family mobility in the Brock and Memorial neighborhoods. The STAY program is designed to educate families about the negative effects of frequent residential moves on children. Mobility rates are quite high in all three project schools — 30 percent at Brock Elementary, 34 percent at Memorial Elementary, and 51 percent at Hogg Middle School. Also, the Read Commission of Houston has indicated a willingness to provide training for volunteers from the neighborhoods in the areas of adult literacy and English as a second language (ESL) assistance. Other local foundations and companies have also shown interest in the project, including Mrs. Baird's Bread Company, the Lyons Foundation, the Marathon Oil Company, and the Southwestern Bell Foundation. In support of the project, these organizations have provided cash grants totaling over $15,000. Representatives from each of these newly involved organizations are also on the project's Partnership Council, approximately doubling the membership of this council.

Future Directions

The further development and support of the school-based Parent Councils will be the major emphasis of the Partnership Council and the project coordinator in the second year. The executive committee will step back and assume a more traditional role as a policy and review board. It is also committed to the strengthening of networks and the development of grant proposals for additional funding to meet identified needs. Attention is also being given to new school offerings such as the accelerated academic programs, additional counseling services, and student assistance programs aimed at the prevention of substance abuse and the improvement of school climate. The widening of existing services into the other participating schools will also be a focus of the project coordinator and executive committee in the second year.

Recognizing that better health care is a priority for these families, efforts are being made by the project staff to involve the Houston Department of Health. More health-related prevention, education, and intervention are urgently needed in such problem areas as sexual behavior and family life education, as is accessibility of public health services. The executive committee has also recognized the need to develop programs for expectant mothers and the preschool population in the project. At present, parents are either forced to stay home with their young or, if they work, must depend on inferior-quality day care for their children. Plans are being developed to offer the Parents as Teachers program (Meyerhoff & White, 1986) to families with younger children.

After reviewing one year of operation, optimism and enthusiasm concerning the School of the Future prevail in the schools. While involving parents in a governing role is a slow, energy-consuming process, the five years of commitment from the Hogg Foundation coupled with the determination of key players in the project assures the eventual success of this empowerment strategy.

References

Houston Independent School District, Research and Evaluation Department. (1991). *HISD District and School Profiles, 1990–91.* Houston: Author.

Meyerhoff, M. K., & White, B. L. (1986, November). New parents as teachers. *Educational Leadership,* pp. 42–46.

CHAPTER 8

A Model for Dynamic Change:
The School of the Future in Dallas

by

Robert B. Hampson, Jacqualene J. Stephens, & Allen R. Sullivan

The decision by the Hogg Foundation to pursue and fund the School of the Future came at quite an opportune time in Dallas. Similar to many large urban school districts, the Dallas Independent School District (DISD) was experiencing significant difficulties—changing demographics, low academic achievement, low teacher morale, increasing student behavior problems, and community pressure to improve the schools. When the School of the Future was offered as a partial solution to some of these problems, the staff of the district was in the process of developing a proposal with similar features entitled Urban Consortium for the Year 2000. The Hogg Foundation proposal was very compatible with the program they were designing. The offer from the Hogg Foundation was timely for Dallas.

The schools selected for participation in Dallas are attended largely by African-American and Hispanic groups and are located in predominantly low socioeconomic areas. Attempting to involve parents was not new to the Dallas district, but several impediments had been encountered in the past. These included a pervasive mistrust of an institution (the schools) which has historically been viewed as autocratic and arbitrary in its attempts to control community children, a sense of powerlessness and hopelessness associated with prolonged poverty, and the tendency of school personnel to think in terms of traditional roles and patterns with respect to student behavior and achievement. Thus, forging a productive partnership with the community was going to be a major task and an overarching goal.

Selection and planning for the Dallas site of the School of the Future project has been subtly yet profoundly different from those processes in the other sites in Texas. From the outset, planning and coordination for the project, as well as the formal proposal to the Hogg Foundation, were orchestrated at the school district level with consultation from key parents selected by the campus principals. Hence, in the Dallas site multiple levels of the school administration, teaching staff, parents, and support services are involved. As will be discussed later, some of the planning and implementation of school-based innovations have also impacted decision making in the district across the board, ranging from movement toward site-based management in selected sites to changes in the way parental advisory boards are utilized in the different schools. These incidental yet broad-sweeping changes are examples of the impact of the project across multiple levels of system organization, yet represent the kinds of results that are seldom attainable in pure quantitative research or program evaluation.

Philosophy and Goals

The overarching philosophy of the Dallas School of the Future project follows those of the Zigler and Comer models and the Hogg Foundation. As noted in chapter 4, Zigler proposed the School of the 21st Century, which emphasizes a holistic and comprehensive approach to child care and education. Quality child care, family support, and parental involvement are key components in any effort to improve our current educational system. Crucial to Zigler's model is the school's becoming the centerpiece of the community, through which a variety of child and family services are offered.

Comer's School Development Program is based on the concept that any successful improvement in a school must occur through mobilizing and involving the community. The theoretical foundation of his work involves a focus on mental health rather than pathology, healthy child development, and a knowledge of systems and their reciprocal levels of influence. However, the most influential concept for the Dallas site to date has been the emphasis on collaboration and involvement of all "stakeholders," including teachers, principals, parents, and students. Comer's ideas have been incorporated into the School of the Future project and have influenced the district to adopt the "Comer Model" in other schools as well.

Going beyond the idea of providing services for specified consumers, and taking a mental health approach to development and education, the Dallas site also emphasizes the healthy development and adaptive alteration of human systems to promote positive attitudes and meaningful involvement of participants. This means that teachers, parents, community leaders, administrators, and students all need to interact. The different systems must learn to adapt and even alter old or unrealistic patterns of behaving. Families can be empowered to support the educational process and to become involved in decision making. Teachers may need to shed negative attitudes about their students and begin to work collaboratively with them in the learning process. Hence, largely speaking, the development of responsive, nonblaming, healthy systems drives this project.

Four major goals have been identified as crucial to the development and eventual success of the Dallas School of the Future.

1. *Decision making regarding education will involve multiple levels of the system, including parents, teachers, administrators, and concerned community members.* The development of three committees at each campus has occurred to provide arenas for input and collaboration from all adults who are involved in the educational process. Known as the School Community Council, the Assistance and Consultation Team, and the Parent Advisory Committee, these committees will begin to address parent and teacher attitudes, develop a closer alignment of expectations, and provide an atmosphere which will encourage and support student development. This collaboration is essential to developing the school into a place that is responsive to community and student needs.

2. *The school will be viewed by neighborhood residents as a positive, essential part of the community.* To this end, the school will be more than just a vendor of textbooks and grades. Planned services for children and their families will impact not only their cognitive and academic development but their social and physical development. The two elementary schools are in a converted shopping center, where there are plans for a wellness center, an adjacent primary health center, a community meeting room and recreational facilities, and other services.

3. *Services identified as essential and desirable for children and families will be easily accessible to families.* They will be housed at the local school building or at least nearby in the community. Accessible services, either with satellite offices in the school building or with computer-assisted coordination of appointments and services at more remote sites, can assist families with scheduling and access to services.

4. *Learning works best in a healthy environment of trust, respect, and enthusiasm.* In many of our inner-city public schools, all of these elements have been lost. Therefore, through open forums and discussion seminars, parents, teachers, and students will meet in response to issues raised by campus teams to share perspectives

and begin the collaboration and negotiation processes characteristic of more healthy systems.

The Key Players

The key players involved in the Dallas School of the Future include the school district, community and parent groups, local academic institutions, and a variety of service and community agencies.

During the initial phase of the project, meetings and planning sessions had been conducted with the district superintendent, two assistant superintendents, four principals, the executive director of site-based management in DISD, the director of student services, and the director of Head Start. Several open houses have been held in the sites for community members and teachers to interact; several teachers from each site have also attended each of these open houses. Hence, the involvement of the DISD has been across levels, involving a top-down structure and involvement in the project.

The coordinator of the project is an experienced and respected social worker in the early education division of special education. Familiar with the schools and community, she has been instrumental in developing trust and collaboration between teachers, parent groups, and the school administration, as well as in coordinating community services that will be establishing facilities in the sites.

Consistent with the philosophy of building communication between community and school and increasing parental involvement in the project, parent consultants and later the parental advisory board have been involved at every step in the planning and implementation of services. Small groups of community leaders (e.g., clergy) and concerned parents from the schools and neighborhoods meet with project staff frequently. Several of these parents were also employed to conduct detailed interviews with a large sample of parents regarding perceptions of community and school. Key community/social service professionals also participated from the inception of the project.

Several academic institutions have been involved in the planning and implementation phases. The University of Texas Southwestern Medical School is represented by an African-American psychologist with extensive experience in the area of child and family treatment and the impact of cultural diversity on the provision of services. She serves as the mental health adviser to the project. As a member of the mental health team she provides training and consultation on mental health issues, problem-solving strategies, and team building.

The Southwest Family Institute provides training for school personnel, using a systems approach that enables them to understand child and family behavior within a community context. In-home counseling is made available to families who would otherwise not seek help, encouraging trust and collaboration with school personnel so that families will see the school as a resource for help.

The School Sites

All three schools are located in the southern sector of the city, with primarily African-American and secondarily Hispanic students. The two elementary schools are situated in a large education complex, a former shopping center now called the Nolan Estes Education Plaza. The physical setting, in conjunction with the modern renovations, provides a roomy, colorful, and well-equipped primary school environment. This complex also has community meeting rooms and considerable undeveloped space which is being used to house the wellness center and many of the community service agencies or satellites participating in the project. In addition, a new Head Start site has opened in the Plaza, largely in response to the School of the Future project and its goals.

The primary school, McMillan Elementary School, covers kindergarten through third grade. The standardized test results from McMillan show scores close to the mean for the Dallas school district. At the end of the 1990–91 academic year the ethnic composition of the 268 students at McMillan was 91 percent African-American and 9 percent Hispanic.

The second elementary school, J. Leslie Patton, is also located in the Estes Plaza and serves grades four through six. Test results from Patton show scores in the lower third for Dallas schools. Ethnic composition of the 223 students at the end of the 1990–91 school year was 87 percent African-American and 11 percent Hispanic with one percent each of Asian and Anglo families. About two-thirds of the students in both schools are on a reduced-cost lunch program.

The third school, Boude Storey Middle School, is located less than a mile from the Estes Plaza, but draws from a larger and more diverse neighborhood. Grades seven and eight are taught here. This school is housed in a large, old, inner-city building, with few of the amenities and without the modern appearance of the two elementary schools that feed into it. Four other south Dallas elementary schools also feed into Boude Storey.

The school has among the lowest standardized scores in the entire district. The ethnic distribution of the 877 Boude Storey children is more diverse— 63 percent African-American, 35 percent Hispanic, and 2 percent Anglo, with four American Indians and two Asians. There is a high proportion of Spanish-speaking families in the Boude Storey district.

The School of the Future project in Dallas will be extending many features of its program into the high school years as well, beginning with the 1991–92 academic year. A four-year grant of $5 million from the U.S. Department of Education will support a comprehensive approach to dropouts at Grady Spruce High School. Special consultation on curriculum and instruction strategies will be provided by the Center for Initiatives in Education at Southwest Texas State University. The goal is to deal with the entire spectrum of psychosocial factors among high school students, ranging from family problems to chronic absenteeism, from illness to child care needs.

Community Survey of Needs: Feedback from the Consumers

Several different surveys and interviews were conducted during the first year to facilitate planning and to collect baseline data.

1. Community residents, both adult and youth, were interviewed by indigenous interviewers trained and employed by the Youth Impact Center.
2. Teachers and professionals in the schools were asked to complete anonymous questionnaires regarding perceptions of the schools, students, and programs (22 were completed and returned).
3. Students in Patton and Boude Storey completed self-esteem and learning attitude questionnaires; a sample of 68 eighth graders and 136 fifth and sixth graders participated.
4. One hundred parents of students in McMillan, Patton, and Boude Storey were interviewed by parents from the project's Parent Advisory Committee.
5. Research associates from the Hogg Foundation conducted key informant interviews with educators, key community leaders, and concerned parents.

In the preliminary survey of the community conducted by youth hired through the Youth Impact Center, 67 interviews were completed, half from adults and the rest from youth. A profile of the neighborhood and parent and youth concerns was derived from these responses.

Overall, the neighborhood surrounding the Nolan Estes Plaza is quite stable, with 75 percent of the respondents having lived in the neighborhood at least 2 years and 35 percent living there over 10 years. Most respondents felt their neighborhood was a "great" or "good" place to live. In terms of suggested needs or improvements, the following services were recommended: more recreational activities for youth, more employment opportunities for teens, better or improved homes, and better police security. The majority of respondents indicated that they "liked" school. Some of the concerns these young respondents had about school had to do with teachers and work ("teachers are mean," "schoolwork is too hard," "not enough clubs to join"), while other concerns dealt more with social and safety issues ("do not get along with classmates," "students steal from each other at school").

One interesting "expectation" was noted when parents and youth were surveyed regarding future plans and perceived ability to attend college. In this pilot sample, 87 percent of the youth in the neighborhood indicated that they planned to attend college after graduation from high school. When teachers were surveyed (by written anonymous questionnaire) on the question of "what proportion of your students have the ability to go on to college," the range of responses was phenomenal, from 10 percent to "all." The average proportion was less than 50 percent, indicating there is some "expectation gap" between students or their parents and many of the teachers in these schools. The only way to begin closing the gap, as Comer has suggested, is to bring all the players together in building the school of the future.

This need to become more involved was clearly indicated in independent interviews conducted later with 100 parents of students in the three schools. Interviews were conducted by parents on the advisory panel and their recruits and paid through a separate small grant from the Hogg Foundation. With very few exceptions, these parents viewed parent involvement in the schools as very low, and all acknowledged that they were not as involved as they should be. Many cited the need to work and other time commitments as reasons for noninvolvement, but a simple majority also cited attitudinal problems as a source on their noninvolvement: "Teachers talk down to us," "There is no one at the school or PTA that speaks Spanish," "I wish someone at the school would call and invite us to come: I usually don't get the pieces of paper from school."

Many indicated they would be willing to work some at school, to participate in voting about school and curriculum, and to contact other parents about the School of the Future and related curricular issues. This is clearly the kind of beginning involvement that the Comer model advocates, and there appear to be potentially willing participants. What needs to happen to get them involved? "Call us," "Get a Spanish caller," "Teachers should encourage us to come to school," "Treat parents like humans."

During the spring term, 1991, before many of the program components were introduced into the schools, an anonymous questionnaire was distributed to the teachers in the three sites, attempting to assess teachers' perceptions of the school, students, and parents. The most universal response from the educators was that parents, though viewed as generally supportive, were minimally involved in the school and its activities. Most cited poor attendance at parent-teacher functions and (in two settings) virtually nonexistent volunteer participation during the school day. The vast majority wanted to see more parents involved more actively, and acknowledged that more creative means of involving parents were needed. Some of their suggestions: "We need to go to the parents," "We need to have alternating day and evening conference times," "We need to give them more advance notice of school activities (maybe even on TV or radio)," "Maybe have a door prize for parents' night."

Many of these teachers' greatest frustrations surrounded the apparent lack of support of the students' families in the learning and disciplinary processes. Many felt that students' attitudes about school and learning would be enhanced if their parents reinforced the values of education and respect for teachers at home. Many were at a loss as to how such attitudes could be reinforced.

From these initial impressions, it is clear that the different sets of participants—teachers, parents, students—perceive some of the difficulties with schools and the learning process from their own vantage points. Parents often feel talked down to and misunderstood by teachers. Teachers feel parents are not involved and, in some extreme cases, are even sabotaging their efforts. Yet all were interested in addressing the issues, and most indicated a willingness to do something about the problems. This process of coming together in a nonblaming problem-solving manner is at the heart of the Dallas project.

One other observation regarding the parent interviews, as conducted by involved parents in this project, and the teacher surveys yields some interesting developments. In a broad sense, these assessments were also beginning interventions. The parent interviewers found some of their respondents very open and willing to become more involved in the project and in their children's school in particular. As the issues were discussed, the sense of empowerment and increasing interest in collaborating for improvement emerged. Over one-third of the parents interviewed have since taken a more active role in their school, having never been approached as a stakeholder in education previously. Likewise, with the teacher surveys, several of the respondents generated novel ideas about how to involve parents, beginning the approach to the middle ground.

Program Components and Innovations

The various components of the services and programs of the Dallas School of the Future are extensive and almost defy listing. In order to simplify the description of these programmatic components, services have been arbitrarily divided into five categories: (1) core innovations, such as the site-based teams of parents and educators and the mental health teams, (2) coordination of community services, (3) innovations in school programs, (4) bringing existing school programs and services onto the school site, and (5) health and wellness programs.

1. Core Innovations. Two important components adapted from Comer's model are the School Community Council and the Assistance and Consultation Team. Both are committees which stress the importance of involving all participants and stakeholders and the necessity of shared problem solving and decision making. The School Community Council is the central component and is comprised of the principal, parent and teacher representatives, and support staff representatives. They meet on a regular basis to develop comprehensive school plans that address academic and social concerns such as school climate, curriculum and instruction, staff development and public relations. The council coordinates all activities and programs at the school and establishes policy guidelines. Thus, any major decisions or policies initiated at the school must be reviewed and consensus reached by the council before they can be implemented.

In the first year of the project, the council has had only a tentative start. It takes time to deal with the novelty of the concepts advocated by the Comer Model and the need for trust to be developed between the participants. As administrators become accustomed to sharing decision making, as teachers perceive their expanded roles beyond the classroom, and as parents are assured that their input is valued and wanted, the development and importance of the council will move along more rapidly.

The Assistance and Consultation Team is a committee that focuses on the psychological well-being of the students and their families. Its primary responsibility is to incorporate mental health principles into the overall functioning of the school. The team is composed of the principal, psychologist, counselor, special education teacher, nurse, reading specialist, resource teacher, and social worker. This committee meets weekly to assign staff to case referrals from school personnel and parents. Individual children are presented in case conference style, with brainstorming about ways to offer assistance or intervention, if appropriate. Issues can also be identified and suggestions made to the School Community Council on policy changes, needs for staff development in a particular area, or needs for additional resources.

Although all of the participants agree on the importance of mental health for their schools, implementing this belief has been more difficult. There have been some "turf" concerns in cases where professionals have been historically accustomed to decision making without much collaboration. Additionally, it has been somewhat of a struggle for team members to think in more creative, nontraditional ways. The use of an outside consultant in the second year will address these issues.

2. Coordination of Services. The project coordinator has been working diligently with community agencies and services to provide services at the school sites. A new Head Start program opened in the fall of 1991 at the Estes Plaza with slots for 80 children, half of whom must be from families in the immediate neighborhood. This program will evaluate its own services, and the participants will be followed through high school. Working in conjunction with the Dallas Youth Impact Center, the project coordinator has also arranged for many services to work directly at the sites, as noted in Table 1.

3. Innovations in School Programs. One major program component that will provide innovation in delivering educational services to children and families is a new cable television hookup. A local cable company has donated $35,000 for installation and maintenance of units in 100 homes that will be linked to McMillan Elementary School by cable. Other funds will be utilized to produce 8–10 hours of programming per week, including school information, homework assistance, parental training, achievement recognition awards, and other content areas identified by parents and educators.

Bilingual parenting classes will be provided for Spanish-speaking families. In addition, the Office of Drug Programs will provide technical assistance and program options appropriate for the needs, interests, and ages of the students. These range from drug education and awareness to actual intervention and reentry services.

4. Coordinating Existing District Programs. Even Start is a grant program that provides a cluster of services to parents of children one to seven

Table 1

New Social Services Being Provided at the School Sites

Agency	Service
YMCA, YWCA	Before- and after-school day care
Juvenile Department	Possible preventive interventions with behavioral problems
West Dallas Boys' Club	Organized recreational activities
Urban League	Job training skills
Texas Department of Human Services	Identification of needs for social services (food stamps, AFDC)
Dallas County MHMR	Identification of children who may need after-school or day treatment programs
Opportunities Industrialization Center	Employment training, motivational counseling, and alternative education systems
Youth Impact Center	Mental health, drug abuse, pregnancy counseling

years of age, and will be available to families in the McMillan catchment area.

Parents are provided materials, toys, and books to enrich early learning. Some child care and transportation are provided, as well as basic health and social services. Literacy training for parents is also provided. An anticipated benefit is the development of strong home-school ties prior to and throughout the child's enrollment in school.

The Homecoming Program returns all handicapped children to their neighborhood schools, providing flexible resources to accommodate student needs on site. This program was implemented in the Dallas sites in fall 1991 and is designed to provide more stability and better communication in home-school relations for affected families.

Adult Basic Education classes are being provided at the project sites to assist interested adults in obtaining high school diplomas through the GED program. Classes will also be offered in Spanish as the interest and need dictate.

5. **Health and Wellness Programs**. Two major programs are central to the emphasis on physical health and wellness of the children and families served by the School of the Future. The first, already in place, is a new physician-based clinic recently opened in the neighborhoods served by the Schools of the Future. The clinic, established by The University of Texas Southwestern Medical School and Parkland Hospital, will serve as a primary health care facility, as well as being an important liaison to the array of other physical and mental health projects delivered to the Schools of the Future.

The second component is a proposed community health promotion project, to be directed by the Institute for Aerobics Research in Dallas. Approximately 1,265 children (and their families) who attend one of the Schools of the Future will participate in this subsidized wellness program, with the general goals of increasing the span of healthy life and reducing disparities in health care among minorities compared to the total population.

To accomplish these goals, the proposed program will focus on three major health-related domains. The first is a general reduction in major preventable disease through education and programmed intervention. The diseases identified as being particularly important for the population served include high blood pressure, coronary disease, stroke, and kidney disease. The second goal is to reduce the risk of disease through exercise and physical activity, for both the children and their family members. Exercise programs and facilities at the school sites will be available. The third goal will be to provide nutrition information and guidance, to reduce incidence of disease related to obesity and cholesterol excess, and to provide nutritionally balanced meals in the schools.

The emphasis will be to promote health awareness and programs for preschoolers through adults (family members) in the school community. The program is targeted to begin in 1992, and evaluation of data will be conducted on an ongoing basis. Baseline data on health (i.e., fitness tests, skin-fold body composition, blood cholesterol levels, blood pressure) will be collected on participants and on matched controls, with periodic reevaluations. The reduction of many of these preventable diseases in this population is the goal, and data collection will continue through the year 2000. Hence, the program is titled "Healthy Families/DISD Project 2000."

Evaluation

As indicated in chapters 1 and 2, research and evaluation are critical components of the School of the Future project. The need to establish reasonable baseline data, temporal comparisons, and adequate controls is central to any evaluation project. In the Dallas site, on-line computerized data on student grades, standardized test scores, attendance, behavior records, and a host of demographic data for each of the campuses were transferred directly to the Hogg Foundation. These data will be available each year of the project. The search for reasonably matched non-program control schools is currently under way.

Hogg Foundation research associates have also conducted several lengthy "key informant" interviews with concerned teachers, parents, principals, and program professionals, following the ethnographic participant interviewing procedure described in chapter 3. A compilation of these results is still forthcoming.

In the spring of 1991, before much of the program had actually been implemented, the local evaluation team assessed fifth and eighth graders (at Patton and Boude Storey, respectively) on a Dallas district-developed measure of student learning attitudes, self-esteem, and classroom climate; a total of 186 students participated. The results suggested that academic self-esteem was largely more positive for the younger children than for the eighth graders, and that students of both ages believed to a great extent that effort and hard work resulted in positive grades and outcome. One of the most consistent findings across age groups was the rated perception of parental versus teacher attitudes ("My teachers think I am smart," "My family thinks I can make good grades"). The vast majority of children at both ages indicated parental acknowledgment of academic ability, but less than half indicated that they "felt smart" in the eyes of the teachers. Classroom climate was rated as more stressful and subject to behavioral disruptions in the older group, but all respondents indicated some lack of trust and a fairly high degree of competitiveness in the classroom. There was no indication from these students that school was a noxious place, but enthusiasm for learning and working was slightly below the district average (based on pilot data from other schools).

In order to attain some standardized assessments of student attitudes and individual adjustment, the Hogg Foundation evaluation staff and their advisors selected three instruments to be utilized across sites: Harter's Perceived Competence Scale for Children, Achenbach's Youth Self-Report Survey (or the teacher rating version of the Achenbach), and the National

Education Longitudinal Study's School Climate Survey. Upper-level administrators in Dallas sensitive to "pathologizing" of the lower-class ethnic groups were opposed to the use of the Achenbach surveys while approving of the other instruments, citing both reactive problems in the youth and community and the possibility that such an approach was at odds with the Hogg Foundation's emphasis upon mental health rather than behavior problems and psychopathology. This latter issue has been an ongoing debate between program and evaluation people from the start in the Dallas site. These concerns appear to have been unique to the Dallas site where the direct involvement of top administrators has resulted in an analysis of the potential impact of selected evaluation activities in a sensitive political environment.

Evaluation is essential to the understanding of the impact of innovations in the schools, including the Schools of the Future. Once the mechanism is in place, the evaluation process should run quite smoothly and unobtrusively in the years to come.

Process and Prospect

Even at the early stages of program development, some impressionistic pros and cons are apparent in the unique top-down structure and implementation in Dallas. Three factors favor such an arrangement, for both pragmatic and theoretical reasons. First, both program and evaluation components have been reviewed and approved at the highest levels initially, since hierarchical decision making was built into the system from the outset. Second, the district and school system as a whole has been impacted by the School of the Future concept, from superintendent and school board members down. Closely associated with the planning meetings for the Dallas School of the Future, the superintendent became interested in implementing two additional programs in the schools, both of which are related to program components of the School of the Future—site-based management for selected school sites and implementation of Comer Model programs in 10 other schools in the Dallas area. Third, parent advisory groups were organized that were interested in implementing new programs across the three sites, rather than on a school-by-school basis.

This community approach (rather than specific campus focus) has paved the way toward larger community needs assessment and a pan-school approach to community problem-solving efforts. For example, at one community meeting related to the project, parents from the catchment area served by the three schools convened to discuss school and community problems and goals. Several African-American parents discussed the unique stressors of Hispanic families, especially with language barriers; several of these parents indicated that they would be willing to learn Spanish as part of their involvement in the community implementation of the program and its parent involvement goal.

There have also been some potential difficulties in this multilevel approach to organization and implementation of the School of the Future. Only time will tell us whether these are outweighed by the positives. Perhaps the most obvious at the start has been the role of the school principals in "owning" the program at their schools. When planning took place at the district level as in Dallas, the principals' role was to select key parent consultants to represent their schools in the planning. The project coordinator has kept the principals involved throughout the planning process, but the issue of investment and ownership appears different in Dallas than in the other three cities. Evaluators of the Dallas site must keep this issue in mind as the process unfolds.

Also in the Dallas site the planning and implementation of research and evaluation has been somewhat different from the other cities. In this evaluation process, district-level personnel, using district-authorized measures of student self-esteem, school climate, and parent/community feedback, collected initial baseline data independently for control purposes. The Hogg Foundation central evaluation team then presented a proposal for a core assessment package to all four Texas sites which would allow cross-site and even national comparisons, including on-line student and school information (attendance, grades, test scores, behavioral/referral data, etc.); district approval was granted at all four sites without hesitation. However, when district-level personnel in Dallas examined instruments that were proposed for the mental health component of baseline data, specifically the Achenbach survey, there was resistance to collecting such information at this stage in the project. Focusing on the potential psychopathology of the lower-income minority groups was viewed as a significant problem. Since this was to be a project involving parents as much as possible, district-level advisers sensitive to minority issues felt that parents would be upset by such inquiry, as they have been in occasional previous research endeavors in the past.

Unlike Dallas, which was striving to develop a closely integrated systems approach, the other three project sites were more likely to have independent service providers coming into specific schools. When the proposal for an evaluation of overall services through certain prescribed instruments was delivered to these sites, relatively little discord or protest was heard. Whether these concerns in Dallas were exaggerated (in terms of pathology versus a positive mental health focus and minority sensitivity) or whether they were visionary can only be determined as time passes. Nevertheless, noting the differences in response to these evaluation issues is important.

Much of what is being undertaken in the Dallas project is ambitious, and project staff have worked diligently to adhere to the major philosophical tenets. These include approaching the school and community from the perspective of a health and competence model, recognizing that all people and systems have inherent competence and integrity, and adhering to the overriding goal of empowering parents and teachers. The Hogg Foundation has provided great latitude in terms of program development and timing, since experience has shown that changing systems through a radical and rapid approach only serves to precipitate crisis and resistance. The emphasis on being sensitive to the community, school, and neighborhood (the critical "port of entry" addressed by Seymour Sarason) will allow the system development to be gradual and recalibratory.

Another important tenet has been the systemic approach to school management, using mental health principles of child growth and development. The school is not viewed as a place where neutral teaching and learning occur, but as an arena for the active promotion of growth, development, and community involvement. Improved student achievement is essential, but so are social competence and psychological well-being. All levels need to be considered—child, teacher, parent, and community.

There is still much to be done. Problems and challenges continue to arise on a daily basis. Future goals now include expanding programming to families with infants, and connecting them to school and community resources as early as possible. Ways must be developed for providing high-quality care for school-age children before and after school. It is also imperative that the site-based teams of parents, educators, and administrators plan with an eye to the future regarding relevant curriculum development and methods of instruction, recognizing the needs of today's children and citizens of the future.

The Dallas School of the Future likely will not be the panacea for all the problems facing public education in Dallas or the urban nation, but it represents a step in the right direction. At least a model and a process for dynamic change, including and involving the necessary key players, has been implemented.

CHAPTER 9

Creating a Sense of Community: The Austin School of the Future

by

Susan Millea & Marion Tolbert Coleman

In the United States social services traditionally are established to serve a particular function, such as prenatal care or substance abuse treatment. Thus a young teen girl with an inhalant abuse problem may be placed in one program. If she is a pregnant student, she is placed in a second, and if a history of child or sexual abuse is identified, she may be placed in yet a third program. But who sees this troubled youngster as a whole person? One need not be an experienced service provider to realize that these problems of child or sexual abuse, substance abuse, and teen pregnancy are very much interrelated as problems of youth and that they affect academic performance.

Answering a Charge to the Community

In many ways the concept of the School of the Future in Austin emerged from community concern that economically disadvantaged families with multiple problems find it extremely difficult to navigate a sea of fragmented social services in which communication between the family, the school, and the treatment program is minimal or nonexistent. Families attempting to gain access to services frequently experience a crazy quilt of programs, all with waiting lists, separate intake procedures, varying regulations, and different eligibility criteria. In addition, these services once identified may be virtually inaccessible due to distance, hours of operation, or cost.

Communities attempting to meet the needs of such families must contend with barriers to agency collaboration, as well. Conflicts in legal responsibility make the sharing of information difficult even when it might reasonably assist a family in need. Funding requirements and service restrictions are the result of a fragmented legislative initiative and policy-setting process which does not address family needs comprehensively. Gaps in the continuum of service exist. There is a lack of community procedures for evaluating the quality and effectiveness of available services and lack of a framework for resolving interorganizational problems in service delivery, not to mention a dearth of adequate preventive and early interventive programs.

The selection of Austin as a site for the School of the Future project seems almost obvious since Austin is the home of the Hogg Foundation. In reality its selection was uniquely related to the activities in preparation for the fiftieth anniversary of the Foundation. In the summer of 1989 the Runaway Youth Case Conference Committee, chaired by the judge of the Travis County Juvenile Court, issued a report highlighting the problems affecting the lives of many children and adolescents in Austin and Travis County. The report called for development of an action plan for Austin/Travis County which should include a "community policy, methods for resource development to fill service gaps, and methods for producing funding for services" (Hogg Foundation, 1990, p. 3). His committee was not alone. The problems of substance abuse, child abuse, teen pregnancy, school dropout, gang violence, and runaways have been and are recognized by virtually all metropolitan municipalities and their service providers.

An outgrowth of the Hogg Foundation statewide Commission on the Mental Health of Adolescents and Young Adults was the formation of a Community Interventions Task Force. This task force was formed in September 1989 precisely in response to the recognition that the problems of children and youth cut across organizational and political boundaries with a need for collaboration and coordination among service planners. The mission of the task force was to identify and address problems of interagency coordination in meeting the needs of youth. It concluded that correction of service delivery problems involves the cooperative efforts of service providers as well as policymakers in both the public and private sectors.

The task force proposed that a Community Leadership Conference be conducted in June 1990 as a demonstration project of how these various stakeholders could work together to provide better services for troubled children and youth and their families. The planners hoped to develop a replicable model for a summit-type conference which would focus on the problems of interagency communication and coordination in service provision. Austin was selected as the site for the conference not only because of its accessibility but also because of the previous and continuing high level of community concern about the needs of multiproblem families.

One goal of the conference was to focus on collaboration across agency lines by helping policymakers experience the kinds of barriers faced by families and direct service providers in obtaining services for children whose problems involve more than one agency. A second goal was to develop a framework of collaboration to close gaps in service provision. Anticipated outcomes included the education of community leaders about the extent of problems facing service providers in trying to coordinate services and a deeper understanding of why so many children are inadequately served.

Planning for this meeting of key community leaders occurred at the same time that a long-term model demonstration project, using the school as the focus for service coordination, was put before the task force for consideration by the president of the Hogg Foundation. While the Community Leadership Conference was perceived as a one-time opportunity to highlight problems of service provision for decision-makers, the School of the Future demonstration project was articulated as an opportunity to demonstrate what could be accomplished over time for children and their families when these goals of integration and coordination are fostered.

Even though the community leaders set the general goals of the School of the Future project, they acknowledged that school personnel should be the ultimate decision-makers, with Hogg Foundation staff serving only as facilitators, so that "ownership" and control would remain at the local level. A number of key persons were identified to be involved in initial planning for both the Leadership Conference and the School of the Future projects. Collectively they provided representation from the local Capitol Area United Way, Travis County Juvenile Court, Austin Independent School District (AISD), Austin–Travis County Mental Health and Mental Retardation Center, the City of Austin, Travis County Human Services, the Texas Department of Human Services Region 6, and the Hogg Foundation.

In October 1989 the Foundation's president met with the AISD director of student support services and the assistant superintendent to present the concept of the demonstration project. The assistant superintendent identified a number of middle and feeder schools which had administrators who might be responsive to the project and could successfully supervise it. By the following month Mendez Middle School and its feeder school Widen Elementary had been recommended for the School of the Future. The schools are located in the underserved neighborhood of Dove Springs, a community beginning to receive attention from the local press due to the lack of out-of-school activities for children and potential for gang infiltration.

The Neighborhood

History. Perhaps the most distinguishing characteristic of the Austin

School of the Future, in contrast to its counterparts, is the newness of the neighborhood and schools in which it is located. One is struck upon first entering the neighborhood with the dense new construction of single-family homes on small lots, duplexes and quadruplexes, and networks of cul-de-sacs. This does not appear to be a "typical" low-income area. Rather, one has the sense of entering a quiet, ethnically mixed suburb of middle-class families. Closer inspection calls to attention a large number of properties for sale or rent, deteriorating privacy fences and rooftops, boarded up or broken windows, weed patches in place of lawns, and gang graffiti. One also eventually becomes aware of the absence of the usual neighborhood small business activity; the community is almost entirely residential.

Dove Springs, perhaps better than any other neighborhood in Austin, graphically reflects the boom and bust of the Texas economy of the last decade. During the early 1980s Austin was among the ten fastest-growing cities in the country. At one time the city led the nation with more than one thousand new residents per month and was listed as one of the ten most desirable cities in the United States in which to live. In 1980 the Dove Springs neighborhood barely existed. By the end of the decade the population was estimated at 20,000 in a 1.5 square mile area. Nearly 75 percent of residents surveyed in 1991 had lived there less than six years. With its newly constructed and relatively inexpensive housing, the neighborhood was attractive to young, upwardly mobile, working families and single parents. This was particularly true for African-American and Hispanic families who migrated from Austin's poor east side barrio area to Dove Springs with the intention of improving their economic status.

During the early 1980s there existed a citywide optimism that the rapid growth pattern in Austin would continue, making the purchase of a home a particularly sound investment. However, when oil prices dropped precipitously and the statewide economy declined, the real estate market collapsed. In as little as 18–24 months, some homes lost as much as 75 percent of their value. Families unable to sell their homes were left with high mortgages, and many faced foreclosures. Concomitant with the economic decline was the cutback in construction and service sector jobs in which many of the neighborhood's parents were employed.

In terms of geographics, Dove Springs is an isolated sector in the southeast quadrant of the city which was developed so quickly that other aspects of community development such as churches, small businesses, recreational space, and health and social services were absent from the design. Only recently has a single fast food restaurant been developed, and it quickly became a focus of social activity.

A survey conducted in the summer of 1990 by a researcher associated with the School of the Future project—canvassing health and social service agencies serving children and families throughout Austin—confirmed anecdotal evidence that no services were being provided in the Dove Springs neighborhood with the exception of the newly established South Austin Youth Services office, a grass roots organization intent on keeping Hispanic youth out of gangs and off drugs. Not only is the community nearly entirely residential, but few vacant areas are available, so there is a significant shortage of both actual and potential office space which could facilitate service organizations entering the community. In short, Dove Springs is a massive, concentrated collection of single new but substandard stock multifamily homes, rental units, thousands of young children, and the neighborhood schools. Moreover, because a number of parents are military or civilian employees of the local air base whose families receive some services through the government, the neighborhood is now further threatened by the impending closing of that base in 1993.

The Neighborhood People. The neighborhood today is a naturally integrated, multiethnic one with a predominantly Hispanic population. The school figures on ethnicity are believed to reflect fairly the area, with 45 percent Hispanic, 25 percent African-American, and about 30 percent Anglo or other. There are also a few Native American families. Asian families are not tracked statistically, but their population is certainly small, if it exists. Both the single- and dual-parent family residents are characterized by the adults working multiple jobs under high stress in order to pay rent or make house payments. Health care utilization patterns reported in a recent community survey indicate a general lack of primary physician care, with high utilization of minor emergency centers and hospitals. The level of health insurance coverage is unclear. Key informant interviews indicate that unemployment, underemployment, and erratic employment are concerns in a number of homes. While there are not a lot of completely destitute families, most are struggling to maintain an upper lower-class or lower middle-class life-style. Family aspirations of using this move to Dove Springs as a step toward upward mobility have been dashed in large part by a changing economy.

Another characteristic of the neighborhood is an apparently unusually high proportion of very young single parents. Sadly, Austin leads the state, and Texas leads the nation, in pregnancies among teen girls aged 14 and under. These young parents are identified by school personnel when the children of these youth enter Widen Elementary School. Another cohort of these young parents is also identified when middle school girls become pregnant. Initial findings suggest that these are two distinct populations since the young parents of school age children are heads of household, while the very young teen parents appear to continue to live initially in their parental homes. One concern recently raised by School of the Future participants was the need to consider development of a support group for grandmothers who are raising teen children and their babies.

Because parents are working multiple jobs or extended shifts, the majority of students (70–80 percent) are latchkey children. Those aged 10–12 are typically caring for younger siblings alone, sometimes until late at night and routinely throughout the day during vacation periods. Some home care is available, but quality neighborhood child care facilities for young children are nonexistent, and they would be unaffordable for most families if they did exist. The School of the Future has responded to this need by initiating an effort to establish a Head Start program at a local church. The lack of space is slowing the effort, but the opening of a program is anticipated soon.

In the migration to this newly constructed neighborhood from one of Austin's oldest and poorest areas, many families have found that a strength of the barrio, the availability of the extended family for such tasks as child care and general pooling of economic resources, is absent in Dove Springs. They indicate that the level of poverty in this neighborhood, though less intractable, is more stressful due to the lack of social supports.

A particular concern of school personnel is the transient nature of families and students in Dove Springs. It is not unusual for a child's home address to change three or four times during the course of a single school year. This mobility is due ostensibly to a pattern of rent skipping and eviction. Even if a family does not move far, if a school boundary line is crossed (which is quite likely at the elementary level), a student may have frequent changes in schools as well. Some children switch back and forth between schools. Concomitant with this pattern is the frequent lack of phone service in the homes, making family contact quite difficult. While community leaders express concern about the sense of rootlessness and lack of cohesiveness this mobility lends to the neighborhood, school administrators, counselors, and teachers voice their concern about the impact of this pattern of family instability upon child development.

Other Areas of Need. The neighborhood first began to be recognized as an area of need in 1987 when school counselors from a South Austin high school began to notice a pattern of disciplinary referrals on students from this neighborhood. High school counselors contacted South Austin Youth Services (SAYS) for assistance. Although SAYS did not include the Dove Springs neighborhood in its service area, that organization proceeded to provide outreach recreational services and eventually was able to open a branch office in Dove Springs in 1989.

Also in 1987, Mendez Middle School was opened. Many of the teachers at the new school had worked with the same students when they attended middle school in East Austin and were familiar both with the problems the students faced and the strengths that the extended families provided in the barrio area served by the East Austin school. These teachers, counselors, and school administrators came into the Dove Springs neighborhood knowing that much of the population of over 1,000 middle school students was at risk for substance abuse, poor academic performance, and/or ganglike behavior.

Community survey information and interviews revealed that parents had long been frustrated by the lack of recreational space for their children and also by the difficulty they had in getting needed attention from city and county decision-makers. The one park serving this community had no plumbing facilities for rest rooms or drinking water. It was and remains the parents' perception that the lack of recreational activities directly results in youth involvement in gangs and drugs because no other constructive options are available.

At the same time that the concept of the School of the Future was being developed with the school district, a joining of forces occurred among active parents, school teachers who live in the area, and SAYS over the issue of recreational space. Local television and newspaper coverage of the plight of the neighborhood was obtained prior to a key election of a county commissioner, as well as the later election of a city council member from the area. The deft handling of negotiations between neighborhood leaders and political decision-makers resulted in the announcement in February 1990 that joint city and county funding had been located to purchase land for construction of a swimming pool next to Widen Elementary.

Parents involved in this initial venture hailed its early success, but they remain leery that their needs have again faded from view with the passing of the election cycle. They are concerned that the community's identified need for a comprehensive recreation-health-education-service center, and not just a swimming pool, will not be realized. Moreover, it may prove to be ironic that the level of press coverage earlier on may effectively leave the larger community with the perception that the needs of Dove Springs have been met. It is hoped that participation of the city council member on the executive committee for the School of the Future will serve to counteract this possibility. Among the community strengths which are being identified along with the needs is the commitment of the stable residents, many of whom are homeowners, to creating a sense of community in the neighborhood. People are reaching out to one another. The neighborhood association is a few years old. A local Optimist Club was formed last year. Residents are learning to use the media to keep the city at large informed of their existence, needs, and progress.

The Schools

The participating schools in the Austin School of the Future are Widen Elementary and Mendez Middle School. Mendez is the only middle school serving the community. Of the four elementary schools in the neighborhood, Widen is the largest and newest. Widen and Mendez schools are across the street from each other and form a focal point of the neighborhood. Indeed their attractive side-by-side facades camouflage the deterioration in the surrounding blocks.

Widen Elementary. This school was built in 1986 to serve a population of 700 students but in 1990–91 had an enrollment of 972. Current enrollment in the program's second year is 1,022 students. It has a total of 36 permanent classrooms and 10 portables. School statistics for the 1990–91 school year indicate that a bilingual program and the English-as-a-second-language program together serve 91 (about 10 percent) of the students. There is a prekindergarten program. Sliding scale after-school care through the citywide Extend-a-Care program is available. In 1990–91, 82 children were enrolled in special education, and 91 were in gifted and talented or honors programs.

The same principal has been with Widen since it opened. In 1990–91 there were 44 regular teachers, 6 special education teachers, 5 special area teachers, a counselor, a part-time nurse, and a librarian. The principal, librarian, and 14 teachers were Hispanic, 2 teachers and the counselor were African-American, and the remaining teachers and nurse were Anglo/other. All were female. Of the faculty, 30 percent held advanced degrees, compared to 40 percent districtwide. This was a comparatively less-experienced staff––36.4 percent having had fewer than six years' experience, compared to 23.8 percent across the district. Teacher turnover in 1990–91 was 20.8 percent compared to 16.2 percent districtwide. These statistics were consistent with interview information that the school attracts new teachers who want access to working with the school district. Reportedly, teachers who transfer out of the school do so primarily because of its location in such a distant point of the city.

Mendez Middle School. This site served 1,039 students in 1990–91. It has 58 permanent classrooms and no portables. No students participated in bilingual programs, but English as a second language was provided for 28 students, or less than 3 percent of the student body. In 1990–91, 133 students were in special education, and 221 were in gifted and talented or honors programs.

Mendez has also retained the same principal since the school opened in 1987. There were 42 regular, 11 special education, and 8 special area teachers in 1990–91. There were also three counselors, two assistant principals, a librarian, and a part-time nurse. In the middle school, the principal, the nurse, a counselor, and 15 of the teachers were Hispanic; 6 teachers and 1 counselor African-American; and the rest Anglo/other. The principal, an assistant principal, a librarian, and 16 teachers were male. Of the faculty, 44 percent held advanced degrees, compared to 40 percent for the district. There were 31.1 percent with fewer than six years' experience compared to 23.8 percent across the district. Teacher turnover was 25 percent compared to the district's 16.2 percent. No reasons for teacher turnover were given, but location is widely accepted as a factor.

The student profiles for both schools appear in Table 1. It is worthwhile to note that data from the 1990–91 school year for Widen indicate that the percentage of low-income children increased dramatically from 51.5 percent in 1989–90 to 69.5 percent the following year and that the percentage of students in attendance for the full year decreased from 81.8 percent to 77 percent during that same period. These two changes highlight the increasing economic stress on families and the problem of high mobility noted earlier. Interestingly, a similar pattern is not seen at Mendez, indicating that perhaps it is the families with younger children who are experiencing increasing stress and also suggesting that the pattern may continue to be seen at Mendez as the younger cohort of children proceeds through school.

Initial Implementation Process of the School of the Future

Widen and Mendez schools are accessible to families and responsible for the welfare of the children for seven to eight hours per day. The school district, recognizing that social and emotional needs affect academic performance and that the school is a logical site for facilitation of social services, has developed a number of model programs over the years designed to address the nonacademic needs of students. Among these initiatives are

Table 1

Student Profile for 1990–91

	Widen Elementary	Mendez Middle School
Total Students	972	1039
% low-income	69.5	50.3
% special education	8.5	12.8
% limited English proficiency	11.0	6.0
% average daily attendance for year	95.5	92.3
% enrolled all year	77.0	84.0
% not disciplined	99.8	82.5
% not dropping out	—[a]	98.2
Ethnicity		
African-American	288 (30%)	258 (25%)
Hispanic	470 (48%)	469 (45%)
Anglo/Other	214 (22%)	312 (30%)

[a] Data unavailable.

the Peer Assistance Leadership (PAL) program; Project Mentor, which pairs at-risk youth with adult mentors; Drug Abuse Resistance Education (DARE) conducted by the Austin Police Department; Adopt-a-School, which invites local businesses to support school needs; the Student Assistance Program (SAP), a broad-based counseling program at Mendez; and a number of in-school initiatives at Widen to enhance student self-esteem. The fact that these programs were already successfully in place in Widen and Mendez schools helped create a positive response from school personnel toward the School of the Future. To some extent the School of the Future is perceived by teachers as an extension of initiatives already undertaken at the schools. However, they also recognize that the School of the Future offers considerably greater opportunity to provide a much broader base of health and social services to the community and to provide the longer time frame believed necessary to create lasting community change.

As a resource, the School of the Future program provides one staff person, a project coordinator, whose primary job is to advocate, negotiate, and coordinate with community service providers to attract community-specified services to the schools. Though the school district is the grant recipient, decision-making authority is vested in the local level, a model which is well suited to the administrative styles of the two school principals. Central elements of the program are the empowerment of school personnel and community members, particularly parents.

Key participants at the inception of the project have included the school district's coordinator of At-Risk Programs, the coordinator hired specifically for the program, both school principals, and identified parent leaders. School personnel have been involved in decision making through the weekly School of the Future teacher committee meetings at Widen and via input from school counselors and the student assistant program team at Mendez. School nurses have also played active roles in the early definition of program components. The initial $50,000 grant from the Hogg Foundation was targeted for the project coordinator's salary, fringe benefits, clerical support, and supplies. The school district's financial contribution includes office space at the schools, furniture, supplies, and administrative support.

Both Widen Elementary and Mendez Middle School staff have identified increased parental involvement as an important goal of the School of the Future. Early focus during the first year has been to initiate awareness of the project among the school faculty, parents, the Dove Springs community, and service providers. This has been accomplished through presentations by the coordinator during teacher in-service training and at meetings of the PTA, neighborhood association, Optimist Club, and local churches. The coordinator also initiated contacts with service providers to facilitate future coordination with the School of the Future.

The principals of both schools have been directly involved in each phase of the planning and implementation of the project and are enthusiastic supporters of it. They have worked directly with the project coordinator to assess the needs of students and to strategize ways of meeting the needs. Formulation of the School of the Future executive committee and the community advisory committee has provided assistance, direction, and focus to the project. Both committees have assisted in identifying resources and community needs.

An early decision was to form a community advisory committee made up of interested parents and an executive committee with membership including parents, school district personnel, a city council member, and service agency representatives. The community advisory committee served as one vehicle for empowering parents in the community. Membership of the executive committee was strategically determined.

Very early on, the community advisory committee recommended that a community needs analysis be conducted. The executive committee acted on the recommendation, and both committees took an active role in development of the survey instrument. Community advisory committee members personally conducted face-to-face interviews. Hogg Foundation staff provided technical support in instrument design, interviewer training, and survey analysis. The survey also served a second function in educating neighborhood residents about the existence of the project. The final activity of this effort will be to report survey results. The project coordinator will present the findings to meetings of community groups and organizations. Because many in the community use the local laundromat, a notice will be posted at this location that the results are available. In addition to the survey, committee members are very actively involved in the implementation of the overall project.

The Price of Milk

Although much has been accomplished through existing organizational structures such as the committees and interagency contacts, a clear cultural aspect to intervening in this community is emerging, especially in working with the parents. The home, family, and friends are the source for meeting one's needs in this neighborhood, and empowering parents means tapping into this resource. Simply put, things do not get accomplished through committee meetings; they occur through interpersonal sharing and visiting. Asking parents to participate in meetings may actually be intimidating to them and ultimately detrimental to the project goals.

When meetings do occur, attention is given to creating an informal, "neighborly" atmosphere. There is an anticipation that children will attend meetings with their parents. Child-oriented activities or child care are organized. Interruptions from children during meetings are not perceived as disruptions, but rather the normal flow of caring for children in the midst of an adult conversation. Food is an important medium of communication. Inevitably, cookies, cake, iced tea, or, on occasion, an entire meal is prepared for participants. Meetings begin with informal chatter about participants' families and only then proceed to the business at hand. In this environment, posting signs or sending home flyers about committees and volunteer possibilities are unlikely to attract a large number of participants. Much more productive is a personal phone call, or better yet a home visit, wherein one identifies which friend recommended this family be contacted and what that parent's particular identified strength is. These methods, like the survey, garner essential input about the needs of the community, its strengths, and parental commitment to participation.

The importance of these methods in building a sense of community, especially in Dove Springs, cannot be overemphasized. With 42 percent of residents having been in the neighborhood less than two years and having come from neighborhoods where families were established for generations, one critical problem in building a sense of community is that residents don't know one another and not many mechanisms exist for meeting. The high degree of ethnic diversity complicates the process. If the School of the Future is to have any long-term impact on the neighborhood stability, this interpersonal outreach may well be the means to establishing it.

While there is some evidence of teachers' belief that parents don't care enough to attend school conferences, it is minimal. Among marginally employed parents the perception of a lack of understanding is exemplified by one parent who stated, "I wish teachers understood that for some of us, taking that one hour off of work for something at school costs us two gallons of milk we don't buy that week." This same person, however, was intent to clarify that most of the teachers are understanding of the situations parents face.

Keen sensitivity to the low self-esteem of unemployed parents who value upward mobility is also critical. School personnel note the positive impact on children evident when they see neighborhood adults working in their school. Clearly there is a desire to involve parents as visible role models at school. On the other hand, interviews indicated that unemployed parents perceive themselves as having nothing to offer and perceive school personnel as being ashamed of them. In this light, parents do not wish to be visible. Unemployed parents who had volunteered in the schools or sought assistance with their children talked about realizing that they are valued. These parents are a vital resource for attracting more parents to the school.

While the needs of families are significant and the ability of families to purchase services is limited, interviews have indicated that parents are offended by perceived offers of charity. If the school is to provide a service for the family, a medium of exchange is needed by which the parent can "earn" participation in the program. One option is to involve parents in specific volunteer activities that encourage a sense of usefulness to the school and help to break down parental intimidation when passing through the doors of the school so that they enter the building with a purpose and something to offer to the school. The parent is a resource to the school and not an individual in need of service from the school.

Outcomes of First-Year Efforts

Contacts with agencies and service providers began at the very onset of the project and resulted in the coordination and development of new programs in the schools. Programs and services were planned with input and assistance from staff of both schools through the Student Assistance Program at Mendez and the Team Leaders' weekly meeting at Widen. The School of the Future was directly responsible for the involvement of 12 community agencies through the schools during its first year. Of the 14 new programs begun, 11 are planned to continue, 1 agency will provide a different service, 1 program is currently under negotiation, and 1 program is in need of funding to continue. The School of the Future provided direct service to 66 teachers, 33 parents, and 244 children or youth during this period. The variety of programs and needs they addressed is reflected in Table 2. While a tally of service programs brought in to the Dove Springs area provides one measure of the success of the School of the Future during its first year, five accomplishments deserve special attention because of their impact on the community.

Recreation Activities. In response to parent concerns that the young people have no recreational space and end up involved in delinquent behavior including ganglike activity, the School of the Future was responsible for negotiating the opening of the middle school gym for a basketball program sponsored by the Austin Police Department's Police Activities League. In addition to providing a recreational activity, the initiative opened the possibility of using the school facility for after-hours activities, created a positive presence of the police in the neighborhood, and involved parents in the school by using them as volunteers in the program. Response to this program was so positive that in the second year the Police Activities League is working to pilot a new program at Widen Elementary targeted at helping older elementary students develop positive responses to negative peer pressure.

Parent Support Program. Another undertaking during the first year addressed the needs of parents whose children are in special education. Concern had been expressed by school staff and project participants that this is a particularly underserved group in the school community. Special needs children whose families are also economically disadvantaged are overrepresented in this population. Using eligibility for free lunch as an index, 39, or 80 percent, of the children were low-income (compared to a school average of 69.5 percent). Also, 53 percent of these children were from

Table 2

School of the Future Programs Initiated in First Year

Program or Service	Agency Involved	Population Served	Number Served
Parent support group	University of Texas	Parents of special needs children	20
Girl Scout after-school program	Lone Star Girl Scout Council	Elementary school girls ages 5–10	50
Sex abuse survivors group	Rape Crisis Center of Austin	Mendez and Widen students in need	15
Recreational program	Austin Police Department and South Austin Youth Basketball	Mendez and Widen students, co-ed, ages 8–15	100
Boy Scout after-school program	3rd grade teachers, special focus troop	3rd grade boys at Widen	10
Stress management training	St. David's Hospital Pavillion	Widen teachers and staff	60
Conflict resolution group	Dispute Resolution Center of Austin	Mendez female students, grades 6, 7, 8	10
Adventure-based counseling	First United Methodist Church	Mendez students, co-ed	10
Cara y Corazon parent support group	Seton East Health Clinic	Spanish speaking parents of students	13
Young animators computer camp	Austin Children's Museum	Widen students, co-ed, ages 10–12	10
Boys Club outreach program	Boys Club of Austin	Mendez and Widen students, co-ed, ages 8–15	19
Heart-to-Heart teen-parent program	Pebble Project for Child Abuse Prevention	Teen parents residing in Dove Springs Community	5

single-parent homes. Of the 49 students in special education at Widen, 51 percent were African-American, 28.5 percent Hispanic, and 14 percent Anglo/other. These compared to districtwide data of 30 percent African-American, 48 percent Hispanic, and 22 percent Anglo/other (Phillips, 1991, p. 58).

Drawing on her previous school district experience, a graduate student from The University of Texas in Austin developed a parent support group which stressed human service intervention as well as educational strategies in order to increase parent knowledge about special education. The group met at the school site and emphasized the role of parental involvement by having the parents identify topics on which they wanted information and encouraging them to help set the agenda. Child care and refreshments were provided, and an informal discussion style was used.

By using the university as a resource, an opportunity was created for increasing both direct service provision in the neighborhood and research related to the overall School of the Future project. Because one goal of this effort was to design a program that could be replicated in other schools, a clearly articulated research component was included in the design of the support group. A survey of special education teachers prior to the support group's initiation indicated, not surprisingly, that the level of parent participation was low, as was parental understanding of both the Individualized Educational Plan (IEP) and the admission/referral and discharge (ARD) process which results in the development of the IEP. Additional questions were directed at teacher attitudes regarding parental involvement and the barriers to such involvement:

- Ten out of eleven teachers agreed strongly that parents could reinforce at home what the school was doing if they were better informed. Eight out of eleven teachers indicated that support and training for parents would make a difference in the classroom with the children they taught. (Phillips, 1991, p. 64)

- Teachers' reasons why parents were not involved were less clear. Five out of eleven respondents indicated that parents lacked interest, and five teachers indicated that the parents themselves had problems which kept them from being involved. Six teachers at least mildly agreed that their own lack of time was a deterrent to parental involvement . . . . When asked what the biggest single barrier was to working with parents of special education students, teachers (most often) cited . . . "getting them to school." (ibid., p.64)

A parent interest survey was also conducted and the results used in setting the agenda. Outcomes of the project included a "how-to" booklet so that the program could be replicated and a simplified manual of parents' rights and responsibilities in the special education process. Though support group attendance was small, an average of 9.8 per session, 8 of those parents came consistently.

Significant improvements in parents' understanding of the ARD process and the IEP were found after group participation. Parents who attended the group were noted by teachers as becoming more assertive and also somewhat more adversarial in the ARD process. Group bonding emerged, and parents began to assume leadership roles within the group. Parents also began to see themselves as possible resources for other special education parents. The group gained a new visibility on the school campus. Though there was not significant evidence that group participation affected the performance or behavior of the children in special education classes during the time frame measured, parents found the group quite valuable and continue to be involved with the schools. During the second year, although the original graduate student is no longer involved, there is enough interest among special education parents to start the group again, this time with one of the original parents co-leading the group. Another of the original parents, whose child has graduated to another school, is advocating for the development of a support group at her child's new school. Truly the goal of parent empowerment is being met here!

Supporting Teachers. While empowering parents has been one method already discussed to meet the needs of children, providing support for teachers is another. The stress level for teachers, especially at the elementary level, is extremely high. Stress management training was provided for teachers at an in-service training session at the request of the principal, who was concerned about the stress for teachers especially related to the high turnover of students in the classroom. Teacher empowerment and support have now taken the form of providing, at the initiation of teachers, a therapist-mediated support group for teachers. All teachers interviewed from both schools in the Key Informant Survey commented about the openness of their administrators to such teacher initiatives. The focus on teacher support services in conjunction with the School of the Future is anticipated to take a reasonably good working environment and make it better.

At Mendez, a shift toward team teaching which occurred during the first year of the project resulted in improved discipline based on reports of in-school suspensions. Although there were some indications in interviews with teachers and the principal that this form of teacher empowerment was mildly threatening to the principal, both teachers and administrators now seem to support the concept. Teaching teams created the use of "in-team suspension" as a mechanism for student discipline which placed a student under the supervision of one of the other team teachers, and kept the student focused on academic tasks. In this way the loss of teacher control of a disciplinary situation, which is experienced when a student is referred to an assistant principal, is circumvented.

Although this shift to team teaching was the result of a change in district policy and not a direct result of the School of the Future, it is consistent with the philosophy of the School of the Future. It demonstrates a shift in control and supports the contention that in this manner teachers develop a more holistic perception of the student in his/her situation. Teacher teams meet jointly with parents in conferences when needed. Teachers interviewed indicated this method did help them and parents understand that a student's problems might not be related to just one classroom situation.

Community Awareness Efforts. In introducing the School of the Future to the parents and community during its first year, a great deal of energy was focused on the development of a community information fair, "A Family Affair." The project coordinator worked with some 40 agencies in Austin providing services from recreation to health and a variety of social services. The community advisory and executive committees had identified this event as a means of informing community families about available services by bringing them onto the school campus for a community activity. Among the agencies represented, a special effort was made with the city health department to provide on-site free immunizations for all family members in need. Food and entertainment suitable for all ages of family members were provided in addition to the information booths. The event also offered an opportunity to begin conducting the planned community needs assessment interviews. Total attendance was estimated at several hundred. The health department had to cease immunizations earlier than anticipated because the response was so enthusiastic. The event appears to be scheduled to continue as an annual activity due to positive community reception.

Partnering with Existing Efforts. One of the requirements of the School of the Future was that the program integrate with services and programs already in place in the schools. At Mendez Middle School linkage was interpreted by school personnel to mean integration with its existing Student Assistance Program (SAP). This program was begun when the school opened in 1987, primarily as a drug prevention program by committed school staff who were aware that many of these students were at risk of developing substance abuse problems. It became unique in the district when it was expanded to include other serious life issues for teens including pregnancy, suicide, sexual abuse, child abuse, runaway situations, depression, conflict resolution, and issues of changing families. This expansion was funded through a demonstration project called Youth in Crisis in 1989–90. One beneficial outcome of this project, cosponsored by the Faulkner Center, Austin Independent School District, and the Travis County Commissioners Court, was the linking of a community-based therapist with the school counselors in conducting group work with the students. This initial partnership served as an introduction of teachers and staff to the potential benefit of the School of the Future philosophy and program.

The opportunity to participate in the School of the Future was perceived by SAP staff as the chance to continue this model of school-community integration and to expand it over a longer period of time than the one-year effort of the Youth in Crisis program, with the potential to create more lasting change in the lives of students and their families. During the first-year effort of the School of the Future, the number of community-based programs involved in the Mendez Student Assistance Program was expanded by about one-third. The School of the Future also helped organize and hosted a Community Forum in the neighborhood in March 1991, when representatives from the U.S. Department of Education's Drug Free School team heard from approximately 25 community service providers about the efforts to develop and maintain the Drug Free Program at Mendez as a community initiative. This effort was acknowledged in the summer of 1991 when Mendez Middle School was named as one of 56 national Drug Free Schools. In conjunction with the award, a group of students, teachers, counselors, the principal, and assistant principal were able to travel to Washington, D.C., for presentation of the award by President George Bush at the White House Rose Garden.

Conclusion

In conclusion, the uniqueness of the School of the Future project rests in its flexibility. It evolves as the needs of the community are identified and changes as those needs change. Thus, the School of the Future in Austin has a distinctly different appearance from counterparts in the other cities.

Though a number of the needs are the same, the newness of this community and its lack of an established social service infrastructure require an approach to community development and school-community linkage that is unique to the character of the neighborhood. The School of the Future is response-oriented.

References

Hogg Foundation for Mental Health. (1990). *Reaching out to youth.* A report of the Commission on the Mental Health of Adolescents and Young Adults. Austin, TX: Author.

Phillips, M. (1991). *A support program for parents of emotionally disturbed and learning disabled children: A demonstration project at the Austin School of the Future.* Unpublished report.

CHAPTER 10

Services for At-Risk and Emotionally Disturbed Children: A Partnership in Austin

by

Deborah J. Tharinger & Kevin D. Stark

General consensus exists that we have failed, through national, state, and local efforts, to meet the mental health needs of emotionally and behaviorally disturbed children and families in our communities and schools. This failure is even more apparent when speaking of disadvantaged children and families. Fortunately, there are indications nationally and in most states, including Texas, that progress is being made, although slowly, in addressing the needs of these children. It has been recommended repeatedly that emotionally and behaviorally disturbed children are entitled to a range of services and that the schools can serve as a central hub for the delivery of many of them. We see the School of the Future in Austin (see chapter 9) as an opportunity to address the mental health and educational needs of disadvantaged children who have serious emotional and behavioral problems, as well as the needs of their families and teachers.

School psychologists are trained to promote the development and learning of all children by working with them directly and by helping to promote the health of the school, family, and community systems that impact children on a daily basis. Promoting the development of disadvantaged, emotionally disturbed, and behaviorally disturbed children and their families is a challenge that requires education and training beyond that usually provided in doctoral school psychology programs. The School of the Future provides an opportunity to enhance the clinical and research training of future school psychologists.

The doctoral school psychology program at The University of Texas at Austin is joining with the Austin site of the School of the Future to create a model training and research center to identify and address the needs of disadvantaged emotionally and behaviorally disturbed minority children, their families, and their teachers. The model program will also provide research and school-based clinical training for the graduate students—future school psychologists. Following the development of locally constructed, research-based, community models for improving child and family competence, children who appear seriously lacking in competence will be identified, studied, and given comprehensive services. In addition, already identified seriously emotionally disturbed (SED) children will be studied and provided, along with their families and teachers, coordinated and comprehensive educational and mental health services. A recently obtained three-year National Institute of Mental Health Clinical Training Grant awarded to the school psychology program at The University of Texas at Austin, which began in January of 1992, supports the bulk of the service component. Funding for a four-year research grant to complement the clinical training component has been obtained from the Hogg Foundation for Mental Health.

A Response to the Mental Health Needs of Children

In the past decade, as Jane Knitzer (1982) has pointed out, there has been extensive acknowledgment nationally of the failure to respond to the mental health needs of the vast majority of our children. It is estimated that at least 12 percent of children and adolescents suffer from emotional and behavioral disorders, and of these at least 5 percent are thought to suffer from serious, incapacitating problems. Environmental risk factors associated with higher rates of mental health problems in children are poverty, minority ethnic status, parental psychopathology, maltreatment, a teenage parent, premature birth and low birth weight, parental divorce, and serious childhood illness (Tuma, 1989). The President's Commission on Mental Health in 1978 reported that low-income minority children were particularly at risk for psychological disorders and behavioral problems because of their low socio-economic status, their often stressful environments, and their lack of access to mental health services. Little has changed in more than 10 years; these children are still disadvantaged by their ethnicity, their poverty, and their social isolation (Children's Defense Fund, 1987). It is estimated nationally that 70 to 80 percent of all emotionally disturbed children are not receiving necessary mental health services (Tuma, 1989), and the figure is most likely higher for disadvantaged children. Multiple and coordinated interventions targeting these children, their families, their schools, and their communities are needed.

The Texas Response. Throughout the 1980s there was debate regarding whether Texas ranked forty-eighth *or* forty-ninth in the nation in per capita spending on public mental health services. Change is needed; fortunately Texas is beginning to address its responsibilities. In the past several years, leaders and concerned citizens in Texas have taken a serious look at the lack of an effective identification and service plan for children's mental health needs, as documented in many reports.[1]

A central concern has been the way allocated monies for mental health services have been spent. It has been estimated that the state of Texas spends $60 million of public money yearly, two-thirds of the total public expenditures for Texas children with emotional disturbance, for residential placements for a relatively small number of such children (Texas State Board of Education, 1991). However, the data indicated that only 25 percent of these children so placed are successfully discharged back into their community. The same report estimated that 50 percent or more of children in residential placements could be served in the community if more accountable school and community-based services were available. The 1989 report on Future Directions for Comprehensive Community-Based Mental Health Services in Texas (Texas Department of Mental Health and Mental Retardation, 1989) acknowledged that children in Texas have traditionally been neglected or underserved by the state's human services system. In response, the report targeted the needs of children and adolescents. The report stated that "to be effective, a system of care for children and adolescents must encompass a holistic approach which . . . includes an integrated system of child-serving agencies with a comprehensive continuum of services which respond to a child's physical, emotional, social and educational needs and includes the education, juvenile justice, child welfare, health, and substance abuse agencies" (p. 61).

Fortunately, significant attention and some financial support from the federal government has targeted as a top priority the development of a coordinated continuum of care across child services. Guided by the Child and Adolescent Service System Program (CASSP) funded by the NIMH, most states, including Texas, are developing systems that will improve and coordinate existing services while creating new services to fill in the gaps. The goals of CASSP include (1) improving the availability of different kinds of care for SED children and adolescents at the community level; (2) establishing mechanisms for interagency coordination to increase levels of collaboration, and ultimately the efficiency of service delivery; (3) developing leadership capacity and increasing priority for funding of resources for child and adolescent mental health services at both the state and the community levels; (4) involving families in the planning and development of service systems, treatment options, and individual service planning; and (5) assuring that service system development takes place in a context that is responsive to the special needs of culturally diverse ethnic groups. As of 1991, one-half of the public school children in Texas are from minority groups (*Austin American-Statesman*, September 7, 1991).

The Texas Children's Mental Health Plan was submitted to the 1991 session of the Texas legislature by the Texas Mental Health Association. The plan is an innovative and coordinated effort by eight agencies to develop and implement an integrated system of community-based mental health care and related services for children with emotional disturbance and their families. The eight agencies include the Texas Commission on Alcohol and Drug Abuse, the Texas Department of Health, the Texas Department of Human Services, the Texas Department of Mental Health and Mental Retardation, the Texas Education Agency, the Texas Juvenile Probation Commission, the Texas Rehabilitation Commission, the Texas Youth Commission, and the Interagency Council on Early Childhood Intervention. The plan has been adopted and funded at a level of $22 million for two years (compared to $2 million for the previous two-year period and no special allocation previously). The plan consists of three parts: (1) community-based core services to SED children; (2) prevention and early intervention, including school-based health and human services for children in elementary schools; and (3) specialized services to SED children in the juvenile justice system. The implementation of this plan represents the beginning of a more positive future for SED children and their families in Texas and reflects a strong philosophy of school-based provision of mental health services as part of the continuum of care.

School-Based Services and the Schools at the Center of Service Delivery. Just as Knitzer's 1982 book forced an acknowledgement and examination of public neglect in meeting the mental health needs of emotionally disturbed children, her more recent book, written with colleagues Steinberg and Fleisch (Knitzer, Steinberg, & Fleisch, 1990), is having a similar impact regarding the failure of school-based and coordinated school and mental health agencies to address the mental health needs of most emotionally and behaviorally disturbed youngsters in the schools. The majority (80 percent) of children and adolescents with serious emotional disturbances and other mental health needs attend the public schools, but children with serious emotional disturbances are underidentified and underserved in the schools nationwide. Knitzer et al. (1990) estimated that only 9 in 1,000 children are classified as SED using the criteria set forth by federal legislation in P.L. 94-142. In Texas only 7 in 1,000 children are so classified (Texas State Board of Education, 1988). The same report also indicated that one-third of the school districts in Texas identify none of their children as SED, while another one-third identify fewer than 5 in 1,000 children as SED.

Those children who are identified and classified as SED typically are provided with special education in the form of resource room or self-contained classroom assistance. These children may be entitled to support services including teacher consultation, school-based counseling or therapy, and family intervention. In reality, educational efforts often fall short, and support services for identified SED children, including services to their families and their teachers, within and outside of the school setting, often are not available and seldom are coordinated. Thus nationally, and even more so in Texas, the vast majority of children with severe emotional difficulties have not been identified and are not being provided with a full range of appropriate educational and mental health services. It is often the lack of resources and services that discourages the identification of these children. The final report of the Task Force on Emotional Disturbance sponsored by the Texas Education Agency and the Texas Department of Mental Health and Mental Retardation (Texas State Board of Education, 1991) recommended that schools be the primary setting for providing physical and mental health services to children and families in the community. Two specific recommendations were (1) that community agencies should be encouraged to provide mental health services in schools and (2) that school counselors, school psychologists, social workers, and nurses should be enabled to do what they do best—intervene and consult with teachers, children, and their families or caregivers. These recommendations are similar to those proposed by Knitzer et al. (1990) that address means to improve the quality of school life for students with emotional or behavioral handicaps.

Other recommendations by Knitzer et al. (1990) of particular importance to the development of the school-based clinical training and research program described in a later section are (1) that efforts be made to prevent the inappropriate identification of students with emotional and behavioral handicaps, including the provision of crisis intervention and other mental health services to all children in schools, the use of effective pre-referral strategies, and teacher and other school staff training; (2) that local, state, and federal efforts be directed at strengthening the policy commitment to enhance collaboration between schools and mental health agencies; (3) that parent support and advocacy groups be formed and opportunities expanded for parents to collaborate in school-related efforts to assist their children; (4) that an adequate supply of appropriately trained educators and mental health personnel be ensured; and (5) that research be conducted that adds to our practical knowledge of the ways in which different intervention strategies affect emotionally and behaviorally disturbed children.

Training of School Psychologists

School psychologists, although often broadly educated and trained in multiple models of child assessment, direct child and family intervention, and school consultation, have traditionally performed within the schools in a much narrower role, dominated by the assessment and placement of children referred for special education. Psychologists in the schools need to be encouraged to create expanded roles for themselves that address the unmet mental health needs of children, particularly those of disadvantaged children. As the schools' role in the delivery of human services changes, school-based mental health professionals are challenged to meet this greater responsibility. School psychologists are central identifiers, providers, coordinators, and administrators of mental health services for children in the schools and as such must be prepared to meet these new expectations. They also must have a working knowledge of services and programs available outside of school for disturbed youngsters and their families, and they must have training and experience coordinating a multiagency effort to provide such services.

In existence since 1965, the school psychology program at The University of Texas at Austin was the first program to be approved by the American Psychological Association, and it has long been considered one of the most outstanding in the country. Graduates of the Texas doctoral program hold more academic and service positions of leadership across the nation than graduates of any other school psychology program. The program gained its reputation by going beyond direct assessment and service models and developing one of the first mental health consultation-based programs of psychological service delivery.

The structure of the program, historically and currently, is based on the scientist-practitioner model of training and practice in psychology. Within this model, scientific inquiry and practice are viewed as complementary and reciprocal in influence. Research informs practice and practice informs research. Both scientific inquiry and competent clinical practice are best served by a firm educational foundation in the behavioral sciences and by heightened awareness of ethical standards and social responsibility.

Acknowledging the breadth of the field of professional training, as well as the range of children's mental health problems that become evident in the school setting, school psychology students are trained in multiple assessment and intervention models across several system levels. The students complete a rigorous and comprehensive training program designed to prepare them to provide assessment, identification, intervention, and prevention services to children and adolescents who are experiencing impairments in the areas of cognitive, academic, social, emotional, and behavioral functioning.

A coherent ecosystemic perspective on clinical assessment, intervention, and prevention links the professional coursework of the program. The current professional sequence of study in the program reflects the increasingly encompassing ecological systems of the child. The professional training program requirements are considered exemplary within school psychology, particularly with regard to the breadth and depth of training and the opportunity for professional skill development with children, schools, and families.

Students are well prepared upon completion of the program. Missing, however, has been a strong cross-cultural or minority mental health perspective. The program is now shifting its focus to addressing the needs of disadvantaged SED children and their families within the schools and through coordinated child-school-family-community efforts.

Additional education and training is needed so that future school psychologists will be better able to evaluate school-based service delivery systems for emotionally disturbed youth, especially those from disadvantaged families. With often limited resources, they must also learn how to create alternative educational and treatment programs that are effective. An important new activity is close interaction with service providers from mental health agencies, psychiatric hospitals, residential treatment centers, and state agencies. Furthermore, at a time when there are inadequate financial resources for children, school psychologists must become advocates for new resources to meet the needs of children and their families. Thus, it is clear that the training of future doctoral-level school psychologists must go beyond the well-established assessment, treatment, and consultation roles within the schools to include family intervention, family outreach and advocacy, interagency collaboration, and access to policy and political process.

Competence as an Organizing Construct in Child and Family Development
The fields of developmental psychology and psychopathology have as one of their goals understanding the nature of etiological, maintenance, and

outcome factors that influence the course of adaptation and maladaptation in human behavior (Masten & Garmezy, 1988). Much of the empirical work in this area has focused on identifying risk, vulnerability, and protective factors, as well as stressors and coping capacities, as children negotiate their developmental pathways. Characteristics of children and their environments (including their families) have been studied with an eye toward the development of effective prevention strategies to promote child and environmental competence.

The construct of competence has been central to the work of such theorists as White (1959, 1979), Garmezy, Masten, Nordstrom, & Ferrarese (1979), and Garmezy (1985). Garmezy's work in particular has been concerned with the identification of factors that cause children to be at risk for emotional and behavioral disturbance and factors that make high-risk children less likely to become disturbed adults. Family variables associated with a heightened prevalence of psychiatric disorders in children have been identified by Rutter (1979) and include severe marital discord, low social status, overcrowding or large family size, paternal criminality, maternal psychiatric disorder, and admission of the child into the care of local authorities. The presence of two or more of these identified risk factors was highly predictive of psychiatric disorder, the higher the number the greater the risk. Rutter also identified a number of protective factors, including positive temperament, being female, the presence of a warm affectionate parent, and a positive school environment.

In a longitudinal study of high-risk children on the island of Kauai, Hawaii, Werner, and Smith (1982) found that the more competent children had better relationships with their parents; enjoyed families marked by parental support, family closeness, rule setting, discipline, and a respect for individuality; had better health histories; and were rated in childhood as active, socially responsive, autonomous, and socially positive. Research findings have described the attributes of competent African-American children reared in social and economic disadvantage to include being socially responsive, active, sensitive, lacking in sullenness and restlessness, intelligent and cooperative, and having positive self-esteem (Garmezy, 1985). Family variables included an active, concerned, involved mother who reinforced her child's interests and goals; an organized home with books; and an adequate and significant adult identification figure. Thus, many studies support positive dispositional attitudes of the child, family cohesion and warmth, and a supportive adult figure as central in the development of children's competence.

Research findings may help us to conceptualize those factors that promote competence in children and that contribute to family competence. Nevertheless, they do not substitute for investigating these factors first hand in the community of interest. To design and evaluate intervention and prevention efforts without first investigating the viability of a model would probably be ineffective as well as scientifically irresponsible. Models of competence in children based on the perception, attitudes, and values of the community would be more appropriate.

Training and Research Center

We have begun four years of training and research activities that have four overarching and concurrent goals in mind: (1) to enhance the lives of emotionally and behaviorally disturbed children and their families; (2) to employ a competence model when designing the investigations; (3) to empower the community by incorporating the community into the design of the prevention, intervention, and special education evaluation programs; and (4) to create a training and research center for our graduate students that embodies a new wave of professional psychology in the schools. To achieve our basic objectives, we have initiated two concurrent and related projects: (a) an advanced school-based clinical training program within the School of the Future, funded by a recently obtained NIMH Clinical Training Grant, and (b) a comprehensive school-based study of the identification and promotion of competence in high-risk and SED children and their families.

NIMH Clinical Training Grant: Service Delivery and Training. To assist us in our efforts to provide mental health and educational services for children with emotional and behavioral disturbances and their families, we have developed an advanced training program that will place a number of school psychology doctoral students, including four NIMH trainees, in the School of the Future. The trainees have been placed in the Austin School of the Future sites for nine months for 15 hours per week. Clinical responsibilities vary somewhat, but in general the trainees have been assigned four SED children at all times, with all case loads consisting of primarily disadvantaged minority clients. In addition, they have been assigned an additional four children who have been identified as incompetent through a procedure described in the next section of this chapter. Furthermore, they are responsible for assisting in developing and conducting a classroom-based prevention program designed to enhance the competence of all children. For each individual case, trainees provide a combination of the following services: crisis intervention; case management; psychological assessment; consultation with teachers, administrators, school counselors, and school nurses; consultation and liaison with professionals from other agencies or treatment facilities; individual or group counseling/therapy; parent education/consultation/therapy (including family outreach services); classroom-based educational and mental health problem prevention and intervention; and child advocacy.

In addition to the NIMH trainees, additional advanced doctoral students are participating in the advanced training program. Their program of study is the same as that for the NIMH trainees, and they have similar applied responsibilities in the School of the Future sites. However, they are required to spend only half as much time providing direct services.

All involved students are participating in an extensive university-based training seminar, university-based clinical group supervision, university-based psychiatric consultation groups, school-site individual clinical supervision, additional university-based workshops and seminars, and agency-based guidance and supervision. The primary topics for the seminar include (1) the provision of school-based mental health services for children and families and (2) ethnic and cultural issues involved in identifying and providing mental health services to emotionally disturbed youth from disadvantaged minority groups. Secondary topics include crisis intervention, provision of home-based mental health services, funding issues, and special topics in assessment and treatment of emotionally disturbed children.

Selected trainees also will complete a three-month, 15-hours-per-week rotation in a state mental health, social service, or education agency or program during the summer. They will focus on working with administrators to learn what is involved in developing multidisciplinary, multi-agency programs and statewide policy and legislation. A number of agencies have expressed an interest in participating in the project, including the Child and Adolescent Services Systems Program, other Texas Department of Mental Health and Mental Retardation programs, the Texas Education Agency, and the Texas Department of Human Services. During their three-month summer rotation, trainees will work on specific projects and cases under the direction of their supervisors.

School-Based Research Program. A four-year investigation is under way to empirically define community models of the competent child and family upon which school-based prevention and intervention programs can then be designed, implemented, and evaluated. The project efforts will initially be focused in the elementary school of the Austin School of the Future, expanding later to the middle school.

Year One. During the first year of the study, focus group methodology is being used. In order to construct community models of competence, it has been necessary to acquire information from various members of the community. The focus group methodology has served this purpose since it has enabled us to get the community involved and to acquire relevant information in an efficient fashion. Focus group interviews represent a qualitative research methodology. As a research method it can precede, follow, or be used in conjunction with quantitative methods. A focus group is a planned discussion group designed to obtain perceptions on a defined area of interest in a permissive, nonthreatening environment (Krueger, 1988). Focus groups typically consist of seven to ten participants who are unfamiliar with each other and who were selected because they have certain characteristics in common that relate to the topic of the focus group. The goal of the focus group method is to provide data on perceptions, feelings, and the manner of thinking of the participants; it is not a goal of the group to reach consensus or decide action. The focus group leader/researcher serves several functions: moderating, listening, observing, and eventually analyzing by induction. Focus group topics and questions are predetermined and sequenced based on an analysis of the situation and data that are being obtained. Thus, the format uses open-ended questions which appear to be spontaneous, but are, in fact, pre-developed. Focus groups have been found to be valid, "if they are used for a problem that is suitable for focus group inquiry" (Krueger, 1988, p. 41).

The focus group methodology is viewed as particularly suitable for constructing models of competence because (1) it permits identification of the vocabulary and thinking pattern of the target audiences (or discrepancies between the various audiences of parents, teachers, administrators, and students); (2) it can provide clues to special problems that might develop in the quantitative phase; (3) it is an appropriate methodology at the planning stages of an intervention; and (4) it stands alone as a research procedure when insights, perceptions, and explanations are more important than actual numbers, as is the case with the identification of a community-based model of competence.

Thus, in the first year of the project, focus groups comprised of parents, students, teachers, administrators, and special education staff have been used to develop community models of (1) the competent elementary student in each of grades K–5, (2) the competent family for an elementary student in each of grades K–5, and (3) the ideal intervention services for incompetent children and families. There were separate focus groups of parents, teachers, and students for each grade level K–5. Thus, for example, the focus groups targeting the first-grade student were comprised of parents who had a child in the first grade, as well as a group of first-grade teachers and a group of first graders.

In addition, given the great variation in the definition of serious emotional disturbance across schools and school districts, a prerequisite to evaluating the current referral, assessment, identification, and intervention process was defining serious emotional disturbance. In order to gain an understanding of the current definition and to develop a community definition, the original focus groups comprised of parents, teachers, administrators, and special educators also met to define serious emotional disturbance for elementary school students. Subsequently, representatives from selected groups met to discuss the current referral, assessment, and identification process, and identified a model system.

A third task was assigned to each of the original focus groups and an additional group comprised of parents with SED children, additional district-level special education staff, graduate research assistants, and one of the primary investigators. This was the development of a description of the community model for an ideal set of prevention and intervention services. Once again, the groups met independently to complete their descriptions and then a larger group comprised of a representative from each group met to develop a composite description. In addition, during this meeting the practical limitations to the ideal model were discussed. Results of this activity helped direct the development of the intervention efforts that will be initiated during the second year of the project.

Year Two. Based on the results of the first year, activities for the second year will include (1) an empirical study of variables that mediate competence; (2) the development of early intervention programs targeted at children and their families; (3) the evaluation of the intervention programs; and (4) the study of referral, assessment, identification, and intervention procedures for SED children. For the empirical study, the composite descriptions of both competent and incompetent students will be used as the templates for selecting subjects. Teachers and administrators will be given the composite descriptions of such students, and they will be asked to use the descriptions to identify the 3 percent of their students (from grades K–5) who are most competent, least competent, and especially average. In addition to these three groups of students, all of the children who are currently labeled as SED will participate in the study as a fourth group. This plan will result in the identification of approximately 30 competent, 30 least competent, 30 average, and 10 SED children. Following parental permission and child assent, these youngsters and their parents will be asked to complete a battery of measures designed to assess the variables that are hypothesized to mediate competence. In addition, the children's school records will be reviewed and included as data in the study.

A prevention program designed to foster the development of the specific competencies that the community considers to be valuable will be developed in the summer between the first and second years of the project and piloted during the second year of the project. An advisory board of parents, special educators, educators, and administrators will be consulted throughout the development process. Students from grades four and five will participate in the pilot program one class period per week during a "special class" period. NIMH trainees and other involved school psychology graduate students will conduct the program.

A similar procedure to that described above for the development of the prevention program will be followed for the development of an early intervention program that will be directed toward the youngsters who have been identified by their teachers as being "at risk." It is anticipated that these will be students from kindergarten through third grade. The program will be piloted during the second year of the project and will be conducted by school psychology trainees.

Also during the second year, based on the community description of the competent family, a training program will be developed by the primary investigators and the school psychology trainees that will be designed to teach the specific competencies of importance to the community. The school psychology trainees will pilot the family training program at the school during the evening. Once again, a community advisory group will be consulted throughout the development of the program. A group of parent volunteers in conjunction with School of the Future staff will promote the program and solicit family participation.

The effectiveness of the prevention, intervention, and family programs will be evaluated by a set of standardized and investigator-developed measures that assess the desired student and family competencies. These measures will be administered to the children prior to their participation in the prevention or intervention programs, and they will be administered to their families prior to their participation in the family competence or intervention programs. The same measures will be completed immediately following completion of the prevention or intervention programs. In addition to these psychological instruments, it is assumed that other naturalistic data such as grades and discipline referrals will be collected before and after participation.

At the present time, approximately 1 percent of the children in the School of the Future sites are identified as SED. As noted in the introduction to this chapter, this figure stands in stark contrast to research that indicates that approximately 12 percent of the children nationally, and perhaps a higher percentage of children in this at-risk population, are experiencing emotional problems that are significant enough to warrant intervention. This discrepancy between the percentage of children who are identified and receive special education services and the number of children who may be in need of special education services raises a number of questions about the special education process.   Some of the broader questions that we are interested in addressing include the following:

1.   What are the current procedures for referring, assessing, and identifying children who are suspected of experiencing serious emotional disturbance?

2.   What special education services are the SED children and their families receiving, and what services, social and psychological, do they believe they need?

3.   What changes can be made to improve the referral, assessment, and identification process so that more of the SED children are identified, and identified at an earlier time?

4.   What is the relationship between the school and families with SED children and, if it is not constructive, how can this be improved?

5.   What is the goodness of fit between cultural factors and the assessment and intervention process?

6.   What are the teachers' attitudes about SED children and their families?

7.   What are the unique psychological assessment and intervention needs of this very mobile, low-income, primarily minority population?

Thus, during the second year, teachers, administrators, special education staff, and parents with SED children will be interviewed regarding the current referral, assessment, identification, and intervention procedures. Permission will be solicited to review the special education files of children who were referred for serious emotional disturbance regardless of whether they were identified or not identified as SED. To help identify the early signs that a child is at risk for becoming SED, the SED children's school and community records will be studied, and complete historical interviews of parents and children will be conducted. The information that is derived from these interviews will be used to help identify children who are currently at risk and could benefit from early intervention. Existing methods of delivering services to the SED children, including coordination of efforts with other agencies, will be examined through similar methods. Current methods for assisting children who are transferring back into the school from a more restrictive mental health or educational placement will also be examined.

Based on these results and the community conception of serious emotional disturbance ascertained in Year One, modifications to the current referral, assessment, and identification procedure will be proposed. If the suggestions are acceptable to school and school district personnel, the proposed changes will be implemented during the second year of the project. The impact of the changes will be evaluated through interviews of special education staff, parents, and teachers of the referred children, and by the number of children who are correctly referred for evaluations to determine their eligibility.

Years Three and Four. During the third and fourth years of the study, based on the results of the evaluations, the prevention and intervention programs will be modified and further evaluated, and the long-term impact of the programs will be evaluated through repeated follow-up evaluations. Similarly, the revised procedures for referring, assessing, and identifying children as SED will be further modified according to the results of the evaluations completed.

Summary and Conclusions

Educators have failed to meet the mental health needs of emotionally and behaviorally disturbed children and their families. Most children and adolescents with serious emotional disturbances and mental health needs attend the public schools. However, children with serious emotional disturbances are underidentified and underserved in the schools. The School of the Future project is designed to address this need by providing an integrated array of health and human services using the school as the locus for their delivery. School psychologists are in a unique position to play an essential role in the delivery of mental health services in the schools. While school psychologists are often broadly educated, their current role in the schools tends to be unduly narrow, dominated by the assessment and placement of children referred for special education. The education and practicum training of school psychologists must be refocused if they are to assume greater responsibility for the school-based delivery of mental health and social services to minority youths and their families. In addition, they must be able to interface effectively with other service providers and state agencies, and to be political advocates for addressing the needs of these children and their families.

The doctoral school psychology program at The University of Texas is joining with the Austin School of the Future site to create a model training and research center. Following the development of a school-family-community model of competence, children and families who seriously lack competence will be provided with early intervention services. In addition, programs designed to enhance competence will be implemented in the regular school classrooms. Services will be provided at the Austin schools by advanced doctoral students in school psychology who will be supported through an NIMH Clinical Training Grant. The research will be supported through a complementary four-year research grant funded by the Hogg Foundation for Mental Health. It is believed that this union of the Austin School of the Future and the school psychology training program at The University of Texas will be mutually beneficial for the community and the doctoral students. In addition, it will positively impact the practice of psychology in the schools.

Note

[1] *Do Kids Count? How Texas Serves Children and Adolescents with Severe Emotional Disturbance* (a 1989 Report of the Mental Health Association in Texas); *Future Directions for Comprehensive Community-Based Mental Health Services in Texas* (a 1989 plan prepared by the Texas Department of Mental Health and Mental Retardation); *Future Direction for Comprehensive Community-Based Mental Health Services in Texas: A Living Plan* (a 1990 report prepared by the Texas Department of Mental Health and Mental Retardation); *Severely Emotionally Disturbed Youth in Texas: Financing and Coordinating Services* (a 1991 Policy Research Project Report from the LBJ School of Public Affairs, The University of Texas); *Report of the Joint Texas Education Agency/Texas Department of Mental Health and Mental Retardation Task Force on Emotional Disturbance, 1988*; *Report of the Joint Texas Education Agency/Texas Department of Mental Health and Mental Retardation Task Force on Emotional Disturbance, 1991, Education and Mental Health: Profitable Conjunction* (Vols. 1 & 2); *Children and Youth with Severe Emotional Disturbance—Problems for Texas* (a 1990 Report of the Task Force on Children and Adolescents with Severe Emotional Disturbance of the Hogg Foundation for Mental Health); and *A Future View of Mental Health* (a 1991 Report of the Hogg Foundation for Mental Health).

References

Children's Defense Fund. (1987). *A children's defense budget.* Washington, DC: Author.

Garmezy, N., Masten, A., Nordstrom, L., & Ferrarese, M. (1979). The nature of competence in normal and deviant children. In M. W. Kent & J. E. Rolf (Eds.), *Primary prevention and psychopathology* (Vol. 3, pp. 23–43). Hanover, NH: University Press of New England.

Garmezy, N. (1985). Stress-resistant children: The search for protective factors. In J. E. Stevenson (Ed.), *Recent research in developmental psychopathology* (pp. 213–233). Oxford, England: Pergamon Press.

Knitzer, J. (1982). *Unclaimed children: The failure of public responsibility to children and adolescents in need of mental health services.* Washington, DC: Children's Defense Fund.

Knitzer, J., Steinberg, Z., & Fleisch, B. (1990). *At the school house door: An examination of programs and policies for children with behavioral and emotional problems.* New York: Bank Street College of Education.

Krueger, R. A. (1988). *Focus groups: A practical guide for applied research.* Newbury Park, CA: Sage.

Masten, A. S., & Garmezy, N. (1988). Risk, vulnerability, and protective factors in developmental psychopathology. In B. B. Lahey & A. G. Kazdin (Eds.), *Advances in child clinical psychology* (Vol. 8, pp. 1-52). New York: Plenum Press.

President's Commission on Mental Health (1978). *Mental health in America: 1978* (Vol. 1). Washington, DC: U.S. Government Printing Office.

Rutter, M. (1979). Protective factors in children's response to stress and disadvantage. In M. W. Kent and J. Rolf (Eds.), *Primary prevention of psychopathology* (Vol. 3, pp. 49–74). Hanover, NH: University Press of New England.

Texas Department of Mental Health and Mental Retardation. (1989). *Future directions for comprehensive community-based mental health services in Texas.* Austin, TX: Author.

Texas State Board of Education. (1988). *Report of the Joint Texas Education Agency/Texas Department of Mental Health and Mental Retardation Task Force on Emotional Disturbance.* Austin, TX: Author.

Texas State Board of Education. (1991). *Report of the Joint Texas Education Agency/Texas Department of Mental Health and Mental Retardation Task Force on Emotional Disturbance. Vol. 2. Education and mental health: Profitable conjunction.* Austin, TX: Author.

Tuma, J. (1989). Mental health services for children: The state of the art. *American Psychologist, 44,* 188–199.

Werner, E. E., & Smith, R. S. (1982). *Vulnerable but invincible: A study of resilient children.* New York: McGraw-Hill.

White, R. W. (1959). Motivation reconsidered: The concept of competence. *Psychological Review, 66,* 297–333.

White, R. W. (1979). Competence as an aspect of personal growth. In M. W. Kent & J. E. Rolf (Eds.), *Primary prevention of psychopathology* (Vol. 3, pp. 5–22). Hanover, NH: University Press of New England.

EPILOGUE: A LOOK TO THE FUTURE

Development and implementation of the School of the Future projects in Austin, Dallas, Houston, and San Antonio have proceeded as originally planned, all things considered. A great deal has been accomplished in the first 18 months of the project, but even more must be achieved in the next two years if the project is to achieve its original goals. As this book goes to press in January 1992, it is instructive to examine critically the progress to date, the problems that must be solved in the immediate future, and the long-range prospects for the future.

With assistance from the Hogg Foundation and its consultants, local leaders in each of the four cities have successfully completed detailed plans for implementation of numerous service components for children and their families. A significant number of the most urgently needed services have already been implemented, while others are slated to start up later in 1992. The coordinators have worked hard to establish new programs for the involvement of parents and teachers as participants in the decision-making processes as well as in the programs themselves. Central administrators in each school district as well as administrators of health and human service programs have enthusiastically supported these efforts. A number of new partnerships involving both public and private organizations have been formed. A major priority for each coordinator has been the securing of private corporate sponsorship. Varying degrees of success have been achieved across the four cities. Efforts must be redoubled in the near future to elicit further support if the original goals of full implementation are to be realized in the next two years.

In each case, the School of the Future project has proceeded in an evolutionary fashion involving many small steps rather than one or two large ones. This kind of building block approach has proven to be particularly appropriate for a comprehensive project of this kind. People must learn to work together in different ways and must build upon existing strengths, a process that takes several years. A key to the success of each project in this initial stage is having as coordinator the right person, an individual who has sufficient knowledge, personal status in the community, and dedication to the key principles underlying the concept to work energetically on a daily basis in achieving the local objectives. The right combination of patience and determination is essential to turn around the distrust, fragmentation, and low morale often characteristic of beleaguered inner city schools and the families in the surrounding neighborhood.

Although each site has adhered closely to the five fundamental principles originally outlined by the Hogg Foundation and has successfully designed and implemented essential elements of the School of the Future, the four project sites vary significantly in many respects. Such variation, both planned and incidental, is highly desirable. Much more can be learned from this kind of program design than from one which is limited to a single site or is comprised of a rigidly imposed model. While valuable in many respects, such variation is particularly challenging from the point of view of research and evaluation.

Standardized baseline data have been collected in three of the four sites, Dallas being the only one that has declined the opportunity to obtain a full set of data on all children in the target schools. The Hogg Foundation has a continuing commitment to support periodic data collection on every child in the four project sites. This will be done for as many years as is necessary to evaluate in detail changes that occur in individual children as a result of institutional changes in the schools and services that are offered to children and their families. Some data being collected are community- or system-based, some are based at the school, and some consist of information about individuals such as teachers, children, or families within the community. Steps have been taken to preserve the confidentiality of such research data, particularly where individual identification is concerned. The Hogg Foundation has assumed institutional responsibility for the safekeeping and eventual analysis of such data.

Throughout the evolution of plans for evaluation and research, the Evaluation Advisory Committee has proven to be essential and will be retained for the remainder of the project. Undoubtedly, there will be some changes in the kinds of data collected, capitalizing upon what is learned in the initial phases of data collection. Feedback from the process evaluation study outlined in chapter 2 has already been invaluable and will continue to be useful in the coming months. Acquisition and storage of the massive amount of baseline data needed for the outcome evaluation studies are well underway. The incentive plans for obtaining assessment data from each child worked well in Austin, San Antonio, and Houston where over 90 percent of the children participated. Fortunately, in those several instances where active consent of parents was initially sought, it was soon realized that this approach would result unnecessarily in a major loss of data, and a shift was quickly authorized by the sites themselves to the use of passive consent as in most of the other schools.

While collection of baseline data has been largely successful, most of the difficult challenges for evaluation and research lie ahead. Of major concern is the likely attrition due to mobility of many families within these poor inner city neighborhoods. A high percentage of families, living close to the edge of disaster from an economic point of view, may be forced to move for financial reasons. An attrition rate of 15 to 20 percent per year is probably tolerable; but if it should rise as high as 30 percent a year, so many children will be unavailable for later assessment that the results of the outcome panel studies based on repeated measures for the same children will be seriously crippled.

The comparison schools appear to be a good match for the experimental schools within each community, at least at a superficial level. Such comparison schools, however, can hardly be considered genuine control units, since they are free to undertake any kinds of program development that are judged to be in their best interest. There is no way to avoid some diffusion, contagion of ideas, or even competition between the experimental and comparison schools. It will be important to obtain more information about new program developments in these comparison schools over the next several years even though there is little that can be done to alter their evolution.

Additional questions remain unresolved but must be dealt with in the near future. To what extent must data be collected on individual families and nonschool members as well as from school children themselves? Can standardized data be obtained from service agencies that have traditionally operated as independent entities? Are the limited staff and resources devoted to evaluation sufficient to undertake the many challenging tasks that must be accomplished in the coming years?

Similar questions can also be raised concerning the steps yet ahead for full implementation of the school reform and integration of health and human services, using the school as a locus for their provision to children and families in the neighborhood. Each of the project sites must expand its project downward to preschool and early infant levels in order to cover the full age range from prebirth services for the mother to age 15. In addition, each site must expand the delivery of such services in order that they are accessible in some form for every child in the neighborhood. Such expansion will require additional resources, will tax the ingenuity of the project leaders, and will require new incentives for parent involvement and self-help. It is still highly uncertain whether such ambitious goals can be achieved within the realistic limitations of talent, resources, and current knowledge. It is even uncertain whether all four sites are now sufficiently robust that they can endure future unforeseen stresses and survive as healthy projects long enough into the future to complete the project's original goals and to evaluate the outcomes of the experiment.

A number of steps to accelerate the pace of communication are being taken by the Hogg Foundation as well as by the school systems and agencies which are the primary partners in the School of the Future project. We are all eager to share what we have learned and to seek advice from others on how best to proceed in the future. This book is only the first of many steps that will be taken to share these ideas. A simple newsletter is being distributed to all of the participants in the four Texas cities. A major conference featuring the School of the Future will be sponsored by the Hogg Foundation in September 1992. It is also anticipated that a number of technical publications of a scholarly nature will emanate from the project and its associated research activity. Regardless of how well the project develops in the next several years, and there is every reason to believe that it has a fairly high likelihood of success, much has already been learned. Such findings will be useful to others elsewhere in the country who are concerned with how best to bring about community renewal, family preservation, and child development using the public schools as a primary locus from which to embark upon reform.